95p

How to Win the
POOLS

How to Win the POOLS

Arthur James

ARCTURUS

Published by Arcturus Publishing Limited
For Bookmart Limited
Registered Number 2372865
Trading as Bookmart Limited
Desford Road
Enderby
Leicester
LE9 5AD

This edition published 1996

All rights reserved. No part of this publication may be reproduced, stored in a retrieval system, or transmitted, in any form or by any means, electronic, mechanical, photocopying, recording, or otherwise, without written permission or in accordance with the provisions of the Copyright Act 1956 (as amended). Any person or persons who do any unauthorised act in relation to this publication may be liable to criminal prosecution and civil claims for damages.

Printed and bound in Great Britain

© Central Press Features Ltd/ Arcturus Publishing Ltd

ISBN1 900032 06 6

CONTENTS

Introduction
Page 7

Simple pools permutations
Page 11

Full block permutations
Page 10

Special perms
Page 19

Introducing Touchline Plans
Page 37

The Touchline Plans
Page 39

Touchline Blocks
Page 111

introduction to the pools

History of the pools

Back in 1918, a Birmingham gentleman by the name of Jervis came up with the idea of a novel form of gambling, based around predicting the results of games of association football played in his area.

He distributed coupons by hand door-to-door and through the local pubs. All of the money staked went into a 'pool' which was then divided up between those who came closest with their predictions. Top prize was around £2.

Various other companies seen the potential for a successful business – including Littlwoods, which was formed by three friends in Manchester in 1923.

Although it initially wasn't a huge success – one week a pools coupon circulated to 10,000 people attracted only a single entry – by the late 20s many hundreds of punters were pitting their wits against the fixture list to try to work out which teams would win, lose or draw.

In 1928 the total pool for one week had reached £10,000, a figure which rose to £200,000 by 1934 and £400,000 by 1939, establishing the pools as a permanent feature of the British way of life.

Now, despite the arrival of the National Lottery, the football pools are still enjoying huge popularity throughout the year.

Every week more than 10 million coupons are entered between the three pools companies, Littlewoods, Vernons and Zetters.

Since many of these coupons are shared entries, around 16 million in this country alone have an interest in the results every week.

Littlewoods, the biggest of the three in terms of payout, gives prizes of more than £205 million every year – that's £4 million a week, or £571,000 per day, £23,000 per hour or £390 per minute.

Basic pools theory

To win the jackpot prize, the objective is to correctly forecast eight games – out of 49 specified games played each Saturday – where the final score is a score draw: i.e 1-1, 2-2, 3-3 and so on.

Each game gets a points value depending on its result:

A score draw counts 3 points

A no-score draw (0-0) counts 2 points

An away win counts 1 1/2 points

A home win counts 1 point

The top jackpot is scooped by correctly predicting eight score draws. The weekly jackpot is therefore won or shared by all those with 24 points (8 score draws), or the maximum possible value that particular week. For example if there are only 7 score draws on the coupon, then the maximum points is 23 (7x3 for the score draws plus 1x2 for a no-score draw).

In a week where there are 8 draws or more, in addition to the jackpot, lesser prizes are paid to those with 23 points, and also possibly 22 and 21 points too.

Payments of lesser prizes depends on the number of draws and the number of winners at each level each week.

Each set of eight predictions is known as a line, and costs a relatively small amount as seen below:

Pools companies: minimum costs per line

Littlewoods: 4/3 pence

Zetters: 1/9 pence

Vernons: 5/11 pence

IMPORTANT NOTE: THESES COSTS PER LINE ARE SUBJECT TO CHANGE. ALWAYS CHECK THEM BEFORE SENDING IN YOUR COUPON

In other words, for just £1.00 you could enter 900 lines with Vernons, 600 lines with Zetters and 133 lines with Littlewoods.

But obviously nobody wants to fill in 900 sets of eight crosses every week. Apart from anything else, there wouldn't be room on the form. This is where permutations, or perms, come in. Perms are a simplified method of entering hundreds, even thousands, of individual lines.

The following chapters in this book describe 30 ways of using permutions to improve your chances to win money. We start with simple full-cover perms, followed by some full-cover block perms, and then move on to the Touchline Plans – mathematical systems, all registered with each pools company.

Each different plan is described in detail, including simple illustrations of how to make your entry and how to check whether or not you are a winner.

simple pools permutations

The easiest way to enter

Simple full-cover permutations are the easiest way to enter any of the pools competitions. As we described earlier, your objective is to pick eight matches from a choice of 49 that are going to result in a scoring draw. If all eight of your guesses are correct then you will win the jackpot – it's as simple as that.

But by adding just two or three extra guesses to the coupon, you can dramatically improve your chances of winning – because you're increasing the number of lines on your coupon.

As explained earlier, one line is eight guesses. But if you make nine guesses, then this is the equivalent of 72 separate lines of 8. This is because there are 72 ways – permutations – of getting 8 separate lines from any selection of nine.

So by just adding one extra guess, you'll be multiplying your chances of winning 72 times.

And the more crosses you add to your coupon, the more permutations of eight guesses you have. The table on the page opposite shows the number of lines you get by entering somewhere between 12 to 30 crosses on the coupon – and the costs with each company you would have pay to enter.

Perm	Coupon Selections	No. of lines	Littlewoods	Vernons	Zetters
Any 8 from 12	12	495	£6.60	£2.25	£0.82
Any 8 from 13	13	1,287	£17.16	£5.85	£2.14
Any 8 from 14	14	3,003	£40.04	£13.65	£5.00
Any 8 from 15	15	6,435	£85.80	£29.25	£10.72
Any 8 from 16	16	12,870	£171.60	£58.50	£21.45
Any 8 from 17	17	24,310	£324.14	£110.50	£40.52
Any 8 from 18	18	43,758	£583.44	£198.90	£72.93
Any 8 from 19	19	75,582	£1,007.76	£343.55	£125.97
Any 8 from 20	20	125,970	£1,679.60	£572.59	£209.95
Any 8 from 30	30	5,852,925	£78,039.00	£26,604.20	£209.95

So if you want to enter, say, 14 crosses on your coupon, the simplest way to ensure that you win if any eight of them come up as draws is to use this simple full-cover perm, with the entry as shown below.

Full Perm Standard Entry		Mark x below A B C D E F
8 from 10	10	
8 from 11	11	
8 from 12	12	
8 from 13	13	
8 from 14	14	X
8 from 15	15	
8 from 16	16	

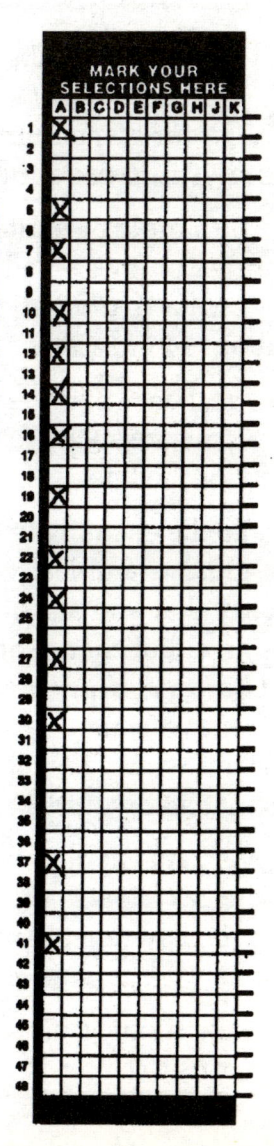

13

full block permutation 1

As explained in the previous chapter, the only sure-fire way of ensuring that you win a jackpot if your given number of selections contains eight draws is to use a full-cover perm.

But as the simple permutations table on page 12 show, the number of lines – and therefore the cost of your entry – escalates dramatically if you want to make more than about 14 guesses.

For this reason, I don't really think that simple full-cover perms are such great value for money. For a start, so many of the lines are wasted.

Let's take the example of the eight from 14 perm used in the previous example. Even though pure statistics might say that any one of the 3,003 lines you entered carries an equal chance of winning, I would disagree. It would be very surprising indeed if the winning line came from your first eight selections, for example. Similarly it would be a shock if you found all the score draws matched your last eight selections.

True, every match on the coupon is potentially a jackpot draw, but my view is that they are very unlikely indeed to be spread symmetrically through your own selections.

So our next method illustrates away of using two full-cover perms to cover 14 matches.

Put very simply, we're just dividing our 14 selections into two groups of seven – the reason being that if these two are chosen independently, then the chances of getting two lots of four in each set is better.

Permutation tables tell us that there are 35 permutations of any four numbers from a group of seven. So by combining two blocks of seven separate entries, we will be entering 35 x 35 = 1,225 lines. Compare this to the full-cover perm figure of 3,003 lines, and you can see how this method represents very good value indeed.

The dummy entry form on the following page shows how an entry should look.

Pools Trivia

A syndicate of four Leicestershire men all refused to believe they had won – each believing one of the other three was playing a practical joke - even when the Littlewoods representative showed his credentials, saying "Anyone can get cards printed!"

Full-block Perm
Entry Guide

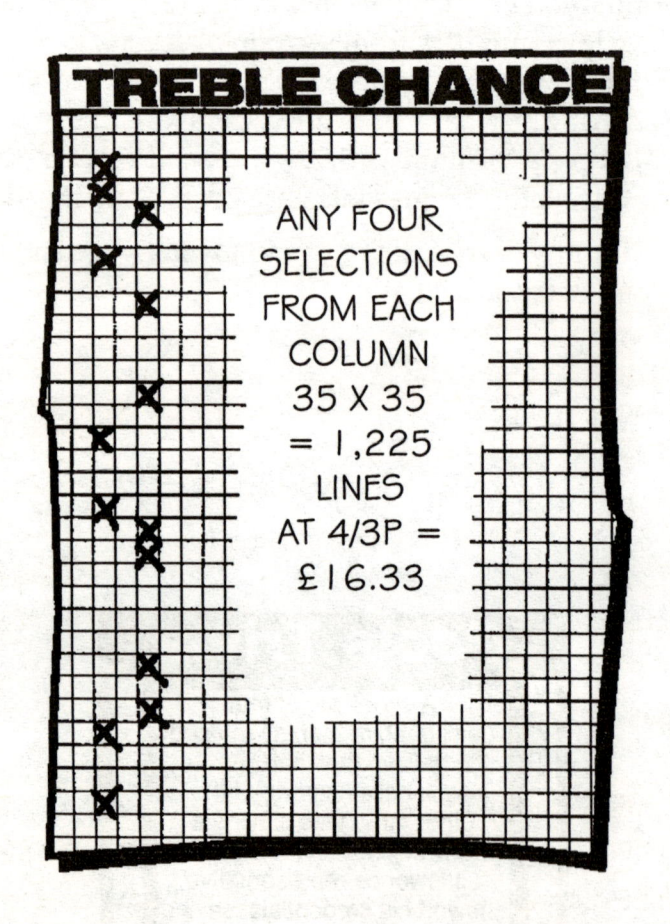

TREBLE CHANCE

ANY FOUR
SELECTIONS
FROM EACH
COLUMN
35 X 35
= 1,225
LINES
AT 4/3P =
£16.33

This is an entry for a Littlewoods coupon at 4/3p per line.
The cost on Vernons would be 1225 x 5/11p = £5.57
On Zetters it would cost 1225 x1/9p = £1.36

4 full block permutation 2

The most frustrating thing about filling in a coupon, I find, is the limitation of the number of crosses that I can afford. If only, I always think, I could afford just one or two more guesses then surely my chances of winning would improve dramatically.

Sadly, in the pools – as in the rest of life – you very much get what you pay for.

However if you fancy having a bit more of a flutter than usual, or if you can persuade a few mates to form apools syndicate with you, then here's a full-cover method which allows you no fewer than 22 selections – giving you a very fair crack of the whip indeed at bagging eight jackpot draws.

Later in the book, I'll be talking you through my cunning Touchline Plans, but for now take a look at this one.

The best method is to divide the 22 selections up into one column of eight, and two columns of seven.

Quite simply, if you get four score draws in any two of your three columns, then you must have a jackpot win.

The diagram on the next page shows how an entry would look.

Entry Guide

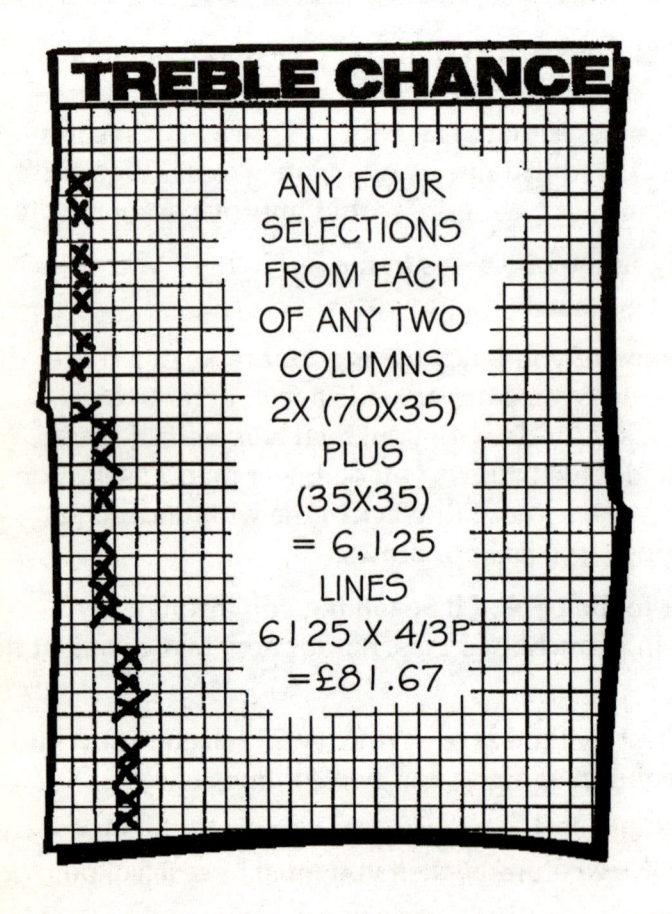

> **TREBLE CHANCE**
>
> ANY FOUR SELECTIONS FROM EACH OF ANY TWO COLUMNS
> 2X (70X35) PLUS (35X35) = 6,125 LINES
> 6125 X 4/3P = £81.67

This is an entry for a Littlewoods coupon at 4/3p per line.
The cost on Vernons would be 6125 x 5/11p = £27.84
On Zetters it would cost 6125 x 1/9p = £6.81

special perm number 1

Enhancing 8 from 10

ONE of the most popular of all Treble Chance entries is a column of 10 crosses to be covered for any eight of them.

There are always exactly 45 different ways of taking 8 from 10, so this full cover perm of any 8 from 10 will cost you 60p on Littlewoods (45 x 4/3p).

Of course, you can always fill in five of these columns of 10 crosses to make up an entry that will cost you £3.00. But it is not always easy to make an exact copy of these 50 crosses on your copy coupon without making any mistakes.

So I suggest that you put all your crosses in one column. That, of course, is much too expensive for more than 12 crosses - but there is a way out.

Put 12 crosses all in the same column and bracket them into groups of six so that you have two brackets as shown in the diagram on page 21.

Copy the instructions alongside and you will have filled in an entry that will cost exactly £3.00 on Littlewoods, £1.02 on Vernons and 25p on Zetters.

You are guaranteed a top dividend plus several minor prizes if you can find any four score draws in each of your two brackets.

There are also many other ways of winning but you usually need at least four score draws in each bracket to be in with a chance.

Checking is much easier, too. If you think you could be a winner, make a note of the 12 Treble Chance values for the 12 crosses on your copy coupon and cross out the two lowest values in each bracket.

This will leave you with eight values. Add them together and you will get the total number of points you have scored with the best one of the 225 attempts you have sent in.

Entry Guide

TREBLE CHANCE

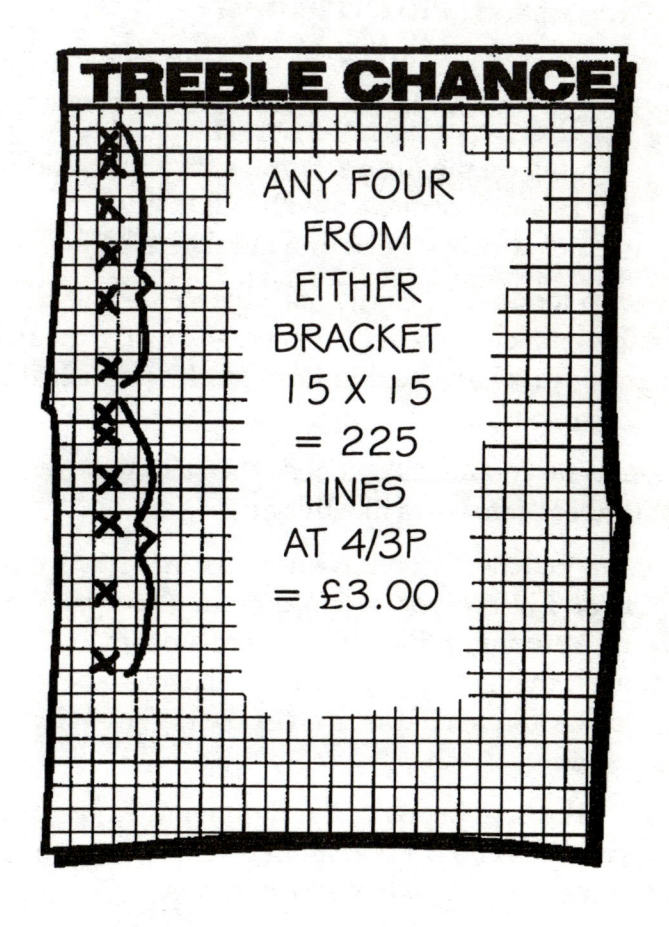

ANY FOUR FROM EITHER BRACKET
15 X 15 = 225 LINES
AT 4/3P = £3.00

This is an entry for a Littlewoods coupon at 4/3p per line.
The cost on Vernons would be £1.02
On Zetters it would cost £0.25

⑥ *special perm number 2*

A Fair Spread

HISTORY never repeats itself. The past has no bearing on the future. If you spin a coin a dozen times and it comes down heads every time, it is still an even chance of a head or a tail the next time.

So it is with football. The only real clue to the outcome of a football match is the recent average form of the two opposing sides, as revealed in form guides published by many newspapers.

But there is no certainty. So choose a system that covers a fair number of matches like this one.

It covers 18 matches of your own choice and it will cost you £2.40 on Littlewoods at one and one-third pence a go; 82p on Vernons at five-elevenths of a penny or 30p on Zetters at their prize plus stake of six goes a penny that pays one and a half times all of the declared dividends.

Put your 18 crosses in one of the right hand Treble Chance columns and bracket them up into groups of three crosses so that you have six brackets.

Copy the instructions alongside to complete an entry made up of 180 separate attempts to win a dividend.

In fact, you must win several dividends including a top one if you get any eight correct score draws in any three of your six brackets.

There are other ways of winning but you usually need at least four correct score draws to be in with a chance. You can easily check your entry to find out.

First circle all correct score draws marked with a cross on your copy coupon and pick out your best three brackets. Note down the nine Treble Chance values for these three brackets and cross out the lowest one leaving you with eight values.

Add them together to discover your best score for the whole entry.

Pools Trivia

A lady winner from the North of England was so overcome when she realised she had won over £3.4 Million the she burst into tears and locked herself in the loo! The assembled press photgraphers were forced to wait until she was talked out of her self-imposed seclusion by the lilting Welsh tones of Windsor Davies.

Entry Guide

TREBLE CHANCE

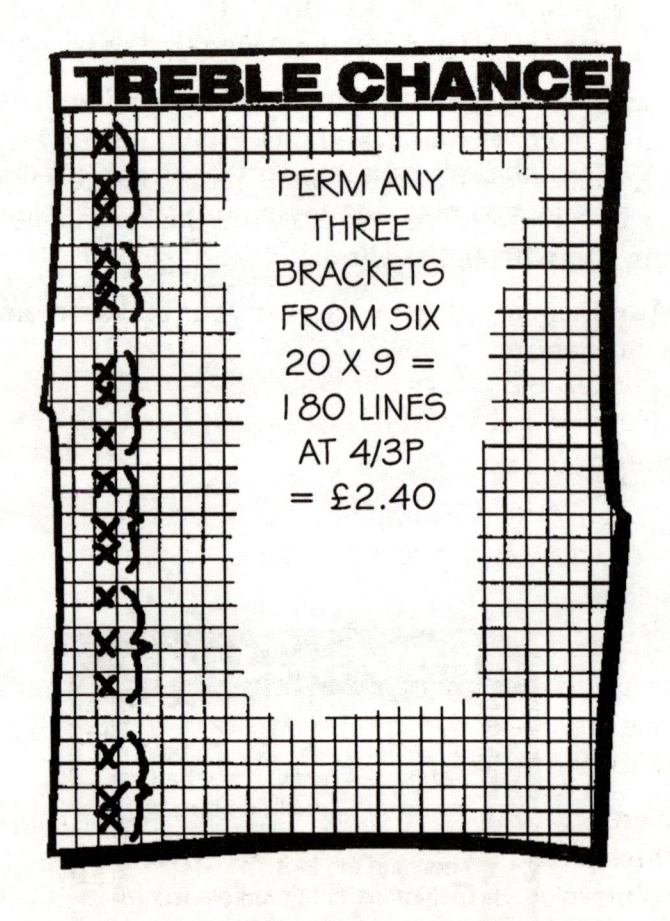

PERM ANY THREE BRACKETS FROM SIX
20 X 9 = 180 LINES AT 4/3P = £2.40

This is an entry for a Littlewoods coupon at 4/3p per line.
The cost on Vernons would be 180 x 5/11p = £0.82
On Zetters it would cost 180 x1/9p = £0.20

special perm number 3

Holiday Week Pools Special

For holiday weeks such as Christmas and New Year, you may find that your pools company is only issuing a short coupon. It is limited to full cover perms and registered plans that can be entered as a single column of crosses.

This form of entry can be checked by computer, thus releasing many of the checking staff for a well earned break.

It is only the winning coupons that get a full scrutiny thus ensuring you that you get everything you are entitled to.

My advice to you is to break up your entry into several columns thus giving you a better chance of capturing one or more of the smaller dividends while you are still in for the big one.

Here is an entry you can try on Littlewoods' coupon for three pounds. Put ten crosses in each of the special columns A, B, C, D and E against your own choice of those games you reckon could end as top scoring score draws.

Also put a cross under these same five letters in the staking box alongside where it says "Full perm standard entries, cost per column 60p, 8 from 10".

The diagram shows you how to do it.

You have now filled in 225 separate attempts for a total cost of three pounds at 4/3p for each attempt.

Checking is quite simple and straightforward. First put a circle round all crosses on your copy coupon that have captured three Treble Chance points for a score draw.

You usually need at least four of them all in the same column to be in with a chance. Pick out your best column. Write down all ten Treble Chance values for that column and cross out the lowest two leaving you with eight values.

Add them all together and you will get the total number of points you have scored with the best one of the 225 attempts you have sent in. If it is a winner, extra dividends are possible.

Entry Guide

Full Perm Standard Entry		Mark x below A B C D E F
8 from 10	10	XXXXXX
8 from 11	11	
8 from 12	12	
8 from 13	13	
8 from 14	14	
8 from 15	15	
8 from 16	16	

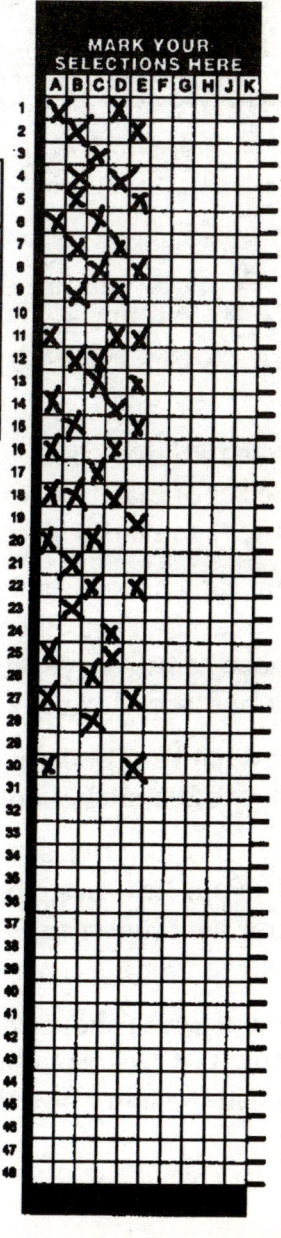

special perm number 4

Machine-gun like rapidity

At certain times of the year we are encouraged to send in single column entries on the Treble Chance pool. They can be checked by machine, thus releasing staff for the holidays.

Take Littlewoods' coupon for example. On the left of the list of matches are the special columns that the computer can read with machine-gun like rapidity.

You can choose from a long list of newspaper plans, but you cannot check them without a chart. Or you can choose a full cover perm, but that gets too expensive for more than a dozen or so matches.

So what I suggest you do for an entry costing £3.60 is to choose 20 matches and arrange your crosses like this.

For your first five selections, fill in columns, A, B and C. Put your next five crosses in columns, A, D and E. Put your next five crosses in columns B, D and F. Finally put your remaining five crosses in columns C, E and F.

The diagram shows you how to do it. To complete your entry, put crosses in the six columns under the letters A to F in the entry box alongside "60p per column, 8 from 10".

Or you can increase your total stake to £4.50 or £6 altogether by using the appropriate premium entry boxes higher up the coupon. You can use this system for a bonus entry on Vernons' coupon. Keep a copy of your entry under the appropriate letters which you will find on your copy coupon.

Checking is quite straightforward. Score draws score three Treble Chance points. You usually need at least five of these top scoring draws to be a winner.

If you think you have a chance, list the ten Treble Chance values for your best column, cross out the lowest two of them and add together the remaining eight values. This will give you your best score for the whole entry.

Claim if you are lucky enough to have scored maximum possible points. Otherwise all dividends will be sent to you without claiming.

Entry Guide

Full Perm Standard Entry		Mark x below A B C D E F
8 from 10	10	XXXXXX
8 from 11	11	
8 from 12	12	
8 from 13	13	
8 from 14	14	
8 from 15	15	
8 from 16	16	

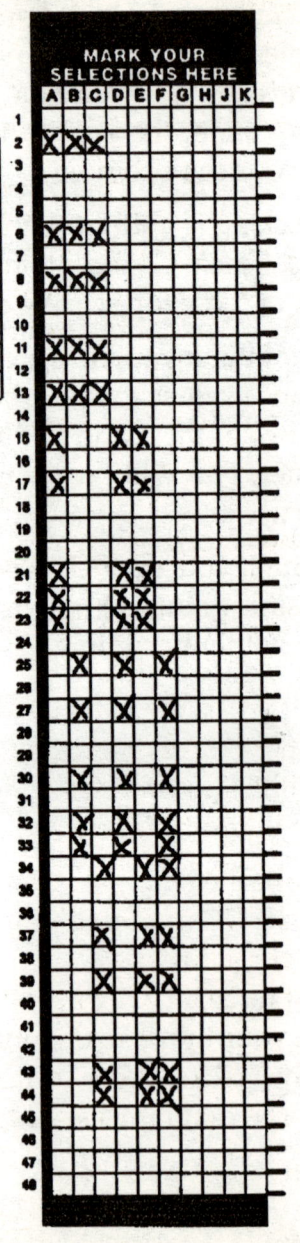

⑨ *special perm number 5*

An Australian Special

Regular pools punters will know that during the summer months, when no football is being played in this country, the pools companies look to the Australian leagues for their weekly fixtures.

One thing I have always noticed is that draws often fall in groups on Australian soccer coupons, and when that happens the pools punter who has bunched his or her selections together stands an excellent chance of reaping the rewards.

Here is an idea to cover 18 selections with a tight guarantee that if seven of your 18 selections end as score draws you will have at least one line with all seven together OR 24 lines or more with six 1-1 draws together. With eight or nine 1-1 draws you will get at least seven in multiple lines.

To make the entry, first decide on 18 matches and mark them all "X" in one column of the Treble Chance (to the right of the fixtures). Then split the 18 selections into six sets of three by drawing a thick, dividing line underneath your third, sixth, ninth, 12th and 15th selections. Finally, bracket those sections of three together into trios. The diagram shows how your entry should look.

Finally, add the following instructions:

"Perm any 3 sets of 3 and perm 8 from 9 = 9 x 20 = 180 lines.

Any 2 matches from each of 4 groups of 3 = 1,215 lines.

Each group of 3 with any 1 of the remaining 5 groups of 3 = 1,458 lines.

TOTAL: 2,853 lines at (add the stake.)"

The cost on Littlewoods is £38.04 which would suit a large-scale syndicate; £12.97 on Vernons and £3.17 on Zetters.

No checking chart is needed with this entry. To check it, simply follow each set of instructions carefully in turn.

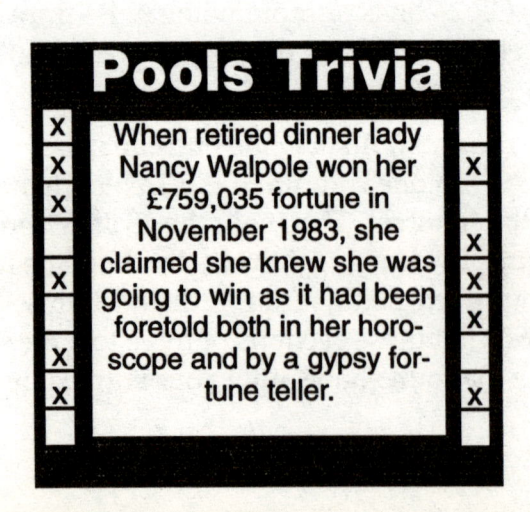

Pools Trivia

When retired dinner lady Nancy Walpole won her £759,035 fortune in November 1983, she claimed she knew she was going to win as it had been foretold both in her horoscope and by a gypsy fortune teller.

Entry Guide

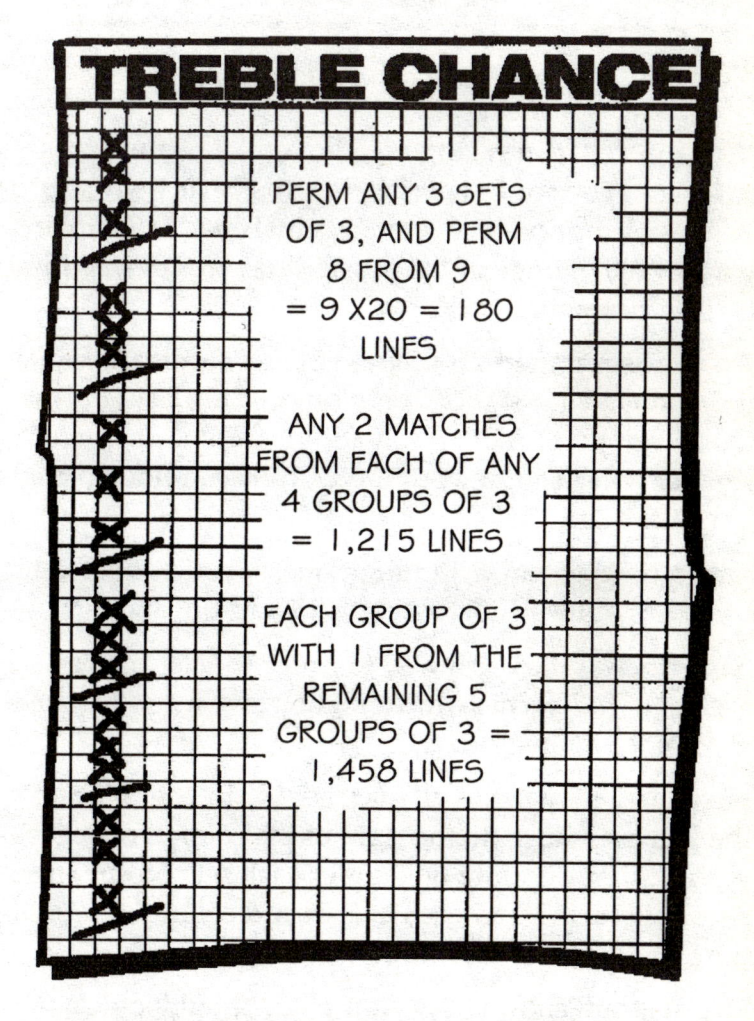

TREBLE CHANCE

PERM ANY 3 SETS OF 3, AND PERM 8 FROM 9
= 9 X 20 = 180 LINES

ANY 2 MATCHES FROM EACH OF ANY 4 GROUPS OF 3
= 1,215 LINES

EACH GROUP OF 3 WITH 1 FROM THE REMAINING 5 GROUPS OF 3 = 1,458 LINES

This entry for a Littlewoods coupon at 4/3p per line would cost 1458 x 4/3p = £19.44
The cost on Vernons would be 1458 x 5/11p = £6.63
On Zetters it would cost 1458 x 1/9p = £1.62

special perm number 6

A series of full perms

The debate has long raged over the relative pros and cons of full perms, in which every single possible option is covered, against conditional plans, where only a range of the possibilities are covered but certain guarantees apply.

An over-simplified summation of this argument is that if you have your sights firmly set on a big jackpot win, then a full perm is definitely for you. But if a series of smaller wins is more your target, then conditional plans have the edge.

The main problem with full perms, of course, is that the cost rises quite steeply as you add additional matches.

Nevertheless, here is a way to cover 18 selections as aseries of full perms which might prove a good launching point for a big prize.

First enter 12 matches all marked "X" in one column of the Treble Chance (to the right of the coupon matches) with a thick, dividing line under each set of four. Then ente r six further matches in a second column and split the six into two sets of three.

The diagram shows how your entry should look.

Complete the entry by adding the following instructions: "Perm any 2 groups from 3 groups of 4 with any 1 from 2 groups of 3 perming 8 from 11 in each case = 6 x 165 = 990 lines at (add the stake)."

The cost on Littlewoods is £13.20 which would suit a syndicate; £4.50 on Vernons and £1.10 on Zetters.

Check by combining any two groups of four in your first column with any one group of three from your second column. This gives you 11 matches which you perm as a full entry of any 8 from 11.

Pools Trivia

Ken Barker, a baker from Swaffham in Norfolk, won £89,246 in June 1983. Just four months later he collected another £46,042!

Entry Guide

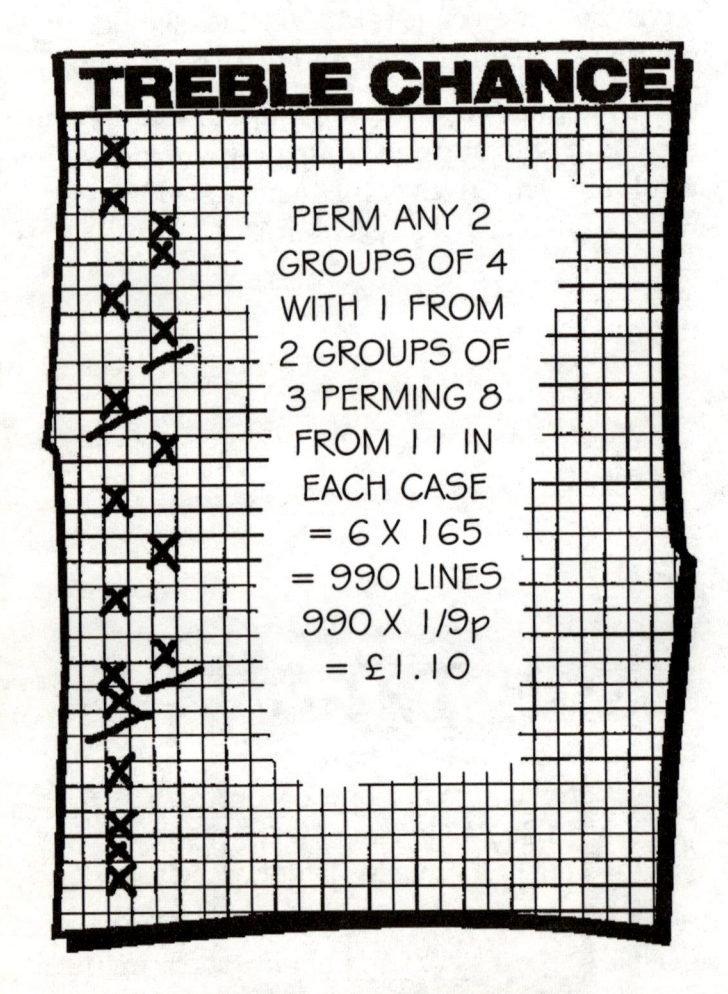

TREBLE CHANCE

PERM ANY 2
GROUPS OF 4
WITH 1 FROM
2 GROUPS OF
3 PERMING 8
FROM 11 IN
EACH CASE
= 6 X 165
= 990 LINES
990 X 1/9p
= £1.10

This is an entry for a Zetters coupon at 1/9p per line.
The cost on Vernons would be 990 x 5/11p = £4.50
On Littlewoods it would cost 990 x 1/9p = £13.20

11 introducing touchline plans

Our first 7 methods of winning the pools have all involved using full-cover perms of one sort or another, meaning that from any set of selections, every single possibility is covered.

In other words if we require eight selections to come up out of any ten, using a full perm means that if **ANY** eight of our ten are correct then we are guaranteed a jackpot.

But as has already been pointed out, there are automatically certain combinations that logic tells us we can pretty much rule out – because of the way draws are likely to fall within the coupon. This means we are wasting lines with a full perm, and that means wasting money.

So how can we be more efficient? The answer lies in conditional perms. These do not cover every single set of possibilities, but can be worked out to give certain guarantees.

For example, a conditional perm covering ten selections could guarantee us seven results if we have any eight correct. This would mean we **definitely** win a minor dividend and **possibly** win a jackpot. So for punters who like to see a steady regular income from their coupons, conditional plans are a great way to go.

I have worked out a whole set of conditional perms which are registered with all three pools companies and are called **Touchline Plans.**

Over the following chapters I'll be showing you how to use some of these touchline plans in different ways to make efficient and cost-effective entries. In each case the guarantees are clearly explained, and checking charts are provided which you can use to check whether you've won a major dividend or several minor ones.

Don't about the slightly strange numbering sequence for these touchline plans – I have registered some 40 of them, but the ones in this book are my favourites, and so aren't necessarily numbered very logically!

IMPORTANT NOTE: All of these following pages give entry costs based on the following costs per line for the three companies:

Littlewoods: 4/3 pence

Zetters: 1/9 pence

Vernons: 5/11 pence

These prices are subject to change. If they do then make sure you alter your entry prices accordingly.

12 *touchline plan number 1*

The Pools Are Different

To win the National Lottery you have to rely on pure chance. The Pools are different. You are in control of your own destiny.

Some numbers are more likely than others to turn up as winners. The clue lies in the predictable form of the teams engaged in the next weekend's matches.

Many newspapers publish form guides which give you a host of statistical information on the various teams playing.

Suppose you wish to stake a total of six pounds in the hope of winning the jackpot of a million pounds plus. Try this system that gives you one of the best chances of winning.

Put 24 crosses all in the same column of Littlewoods' full coupon (not the short coupon) against the 24 games you judge as having the best chance.

Bracket them up into groups of four crosses so that you have six brackets. Copy the instructions alongside as shown in the diagram to complete your entry.

You have now filled in six entries of Touch-Line Plan No. 1.

This means that if you get eight score draws in any four brackets, one of the 450 attempts you have sent in will include at least six of them, possibly seven or with luck even all eight.

You can send in the same system on Vernons' coupon at 5/11ths of a penny for a total of £2.05. Zetters' total stake at nine goes a penny is just 50 pence.

For a quick check, first refer to the Treble Chance checklist published over the weekend and circle all crosses on your copy coupon that have scored the maximum of three points for a score draw.

Now pick out your best four brackets. List the sixteen Treble Chance scores for these four brackets in correct coupon order down the side of the full plan checking table on the page overleaf.

You can now count up the total number of points you have scored with the eight crosses in each one of the 30 columns of the plan to see if any of them are winners.

Dividends are usually paid down to 21 points.

Touchline Plan No. 1: Entry Guide

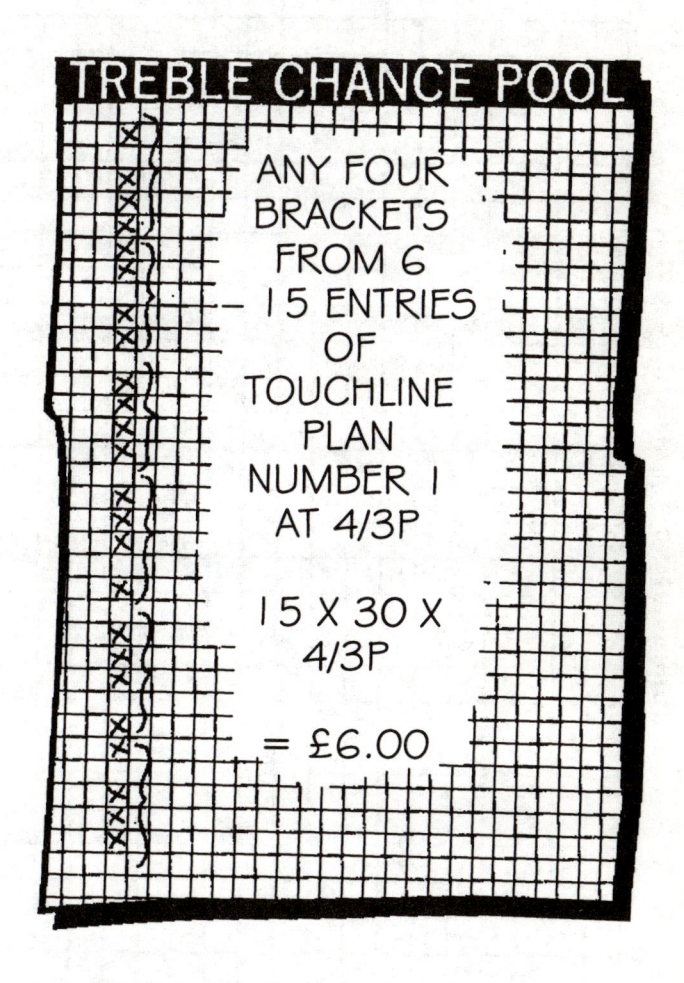

TREBLE CHANCE POOL

ANY FOUR BRACKETS FROM 6

15 ENTRIES OF TOUCHLINE PLAN NUMBER 1 AT 4/3P

15 X 30 X 4/3P

= £6.00

This is an entry for a Littlewoods coupon at 4/3p per line.
The cost on Vernons would be 450 x 5/11p = £2.05
On Zetters it would cost 450 x1/9p = £0.50

Touchline Plan No. 1 Checking Chart

Results	1	2	3	4	5	6	7	8	9	10	11	12	13	14	15	16	17	18	19	20	21	22	23	24	25	26	27	28	29	30
	X	X	X	X	X	X																								
		X	X	X	X		X																							
			X	X																										
			X					X	X																					
				X	X			X	X	X																				
								X	X	X	X																			
						X	X	X	X			X	X																	
						X	X					X	X	X																
							X	X		X	X	X	X	X	X	X	X													
									X						X	X	X	X	X											
		X	X				X	X			X			X	X		X	X	X	X	X									
				X	X	X												X	X	X	X		X	X		X				
																						X	X	X	X	X	X			
												X	X	X	X		X	X		X		X	X		X	X	X	X		X
			X	X	X			X		X		X	X	X	X		X	X	X		X			X	X		X	X	X	
			X	X	X	X	X	X	X	X	X			X	X	X		X	X	X			X							
Points																														

touchline plan number 2

Top Value For Your Money

Readers sometimes write and tell me that they want to extract from the pools as much value for money as they possibly can.

I tell them to cover as many matches as possible for as low a stake as possible with a single column multiple plan that is as perfect as possible.

Here for example is a way of covering no fewer than thirty matches on Zetters' Treble Chance pool for £2.80 at nine goes a penny (£4.20 at six goes a penny, £11.45 on Vernons' coupon at 5/11ths of a penny a go or £33.60 on Littlewoods' at 1-1/3rd pence).

Put 30 crosses all in the same column against the 30 games you have chosen as possible score draws that score the maximum of three Treble Chance points.

Bracket them into groups of three crosses so that you have ten brackets. Copy the instructions alongside as shown in the specimen entry. You have now filled in 210 entries of Touch-Line Plan No. 2, a total of 2,520 attempts.

You must win a top dividend (and it could be a big one) if you succeed in getting any ten score draws in any four of your ten brackets. There are many other ways of winning dividends.

There is no need to check all 2,520 attempts or anything like it. Indeed you only need to check twelve of them.

Refer to the Treble Chance check published over the weekend. First circle all crosses on your copy coupon that have captured three points for a score draw.

If you think you could be a winner, pick out your best four brackets. List the twelve Treble Chance values for these four brackets down the side of the full plan on page 46.

You now need only to count up the total number of points you have scored with the eight crosses in each one of the twelve columns of the plan to find out whether or not you are likely to have won anything.

You can use this plan any week throughout the year but as in includes brackets it is not suitable for a standing entry covering the same match numbers for more than a single week.

Touchline Plan No. 2: Entry Guide

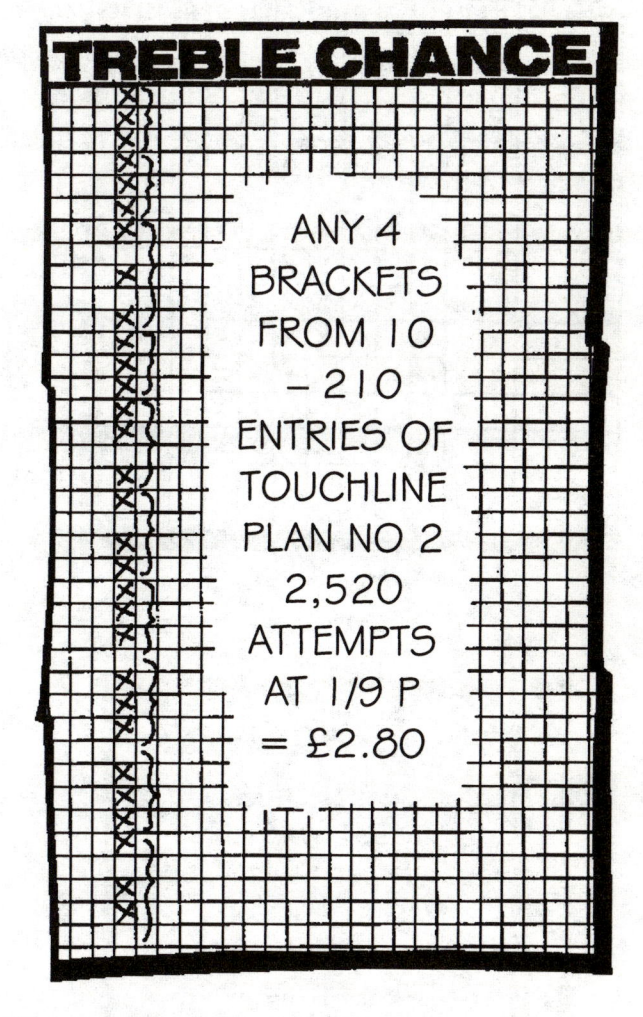

TREBLE CHANCE

ANY 4 BRACKETS FROM 10 – 210 ENTRIES OF TOUCHLINE PLAN NO 2 2,520 ATTEMPTS AT 1/9 P = £2.80

This is an entry for a Zetters coupon at 1/9p per line.
The cost on Littlewoods would be 2,520 x 4/3p = £33.60
On Vernons it would cost 2,520 x 5/11p = £11.46

Touchline Plan No. 2 Checking Chart

Results	1	2	3	4	5	6	7	8	9	10	11	12
	X			X	X		X			X	X	X	X
		X	X			X	X		X			X	X	X
		X	X	X			X	X		X			X	X
		X	X	X	X			X	X		X			X
		X	X	X	X	X			X	X		X		
			X	X	X	X	X			X	X			X
	X			X	X	X	X	X			X	X		
		X			X	X	X	X	X			X	X	
	X		X			X	X	X	X	X			X	
	X	X			X			X	X	X	X	X		
		X	X			X			X	X	X	X	X	
			X	X			X			X	X	X	X	X
Points												

Pools Trivia

Coincidence struck in March 1984, when three separate people scooped first dividends on Littlewoods Pools. Their names were Gamble, Luck and Riches!

touchline plan number 5

Use Your Skill To Win A Million

You can use your skill with this neat little plan to bring you closer to that multi-million pound dream. The pools are so easy. You just put a few crosses in a column with appropriate instructions and wait for the weekend. You can check for yourself as soon as the football results come out. All winners are paid within a few days without claiming.

Here is a way of playing Littlewoods' jackpot Treble Chance for as little as £2.28 a week. Use their long coupon (not the short one).

Put 18 crosses in one of the columns to the right of the list of matches and bracket them into three sixes. Copy the instructions alongside as shown in the example. You have now filled in 171 attempts.

You will win a top dividend (and it could be a big one) whenever you get any nine correct scoring draws (1-1, 2-2 etc.) in any two of your three brackets.

There are many other ways of winning one or more of the several dividends paid every week.

You usually need at least four correct score draws to be a winner. To find out, refer to the Treble Chance check published widely over the weekend. Circle all crosses on your copy coupon that have scored three points for a score draw and pick out your best two brackets.

List these 12 Treble Chance values down the side of all three sections of Touch-Line Plan No. 5 which appears in full on this page.

You can now count up the total number of points you have scored with the eight crosses in each one of the 57 columns of the plan to find out if any of them are winners.

On Vernons' coupon at 5/11ths of a penny a go, this entry will cost you 78 pence. On Zetters at nine goes a penny the total stake is 19 pence.

Touchline Plan No. 5: Entry Guide

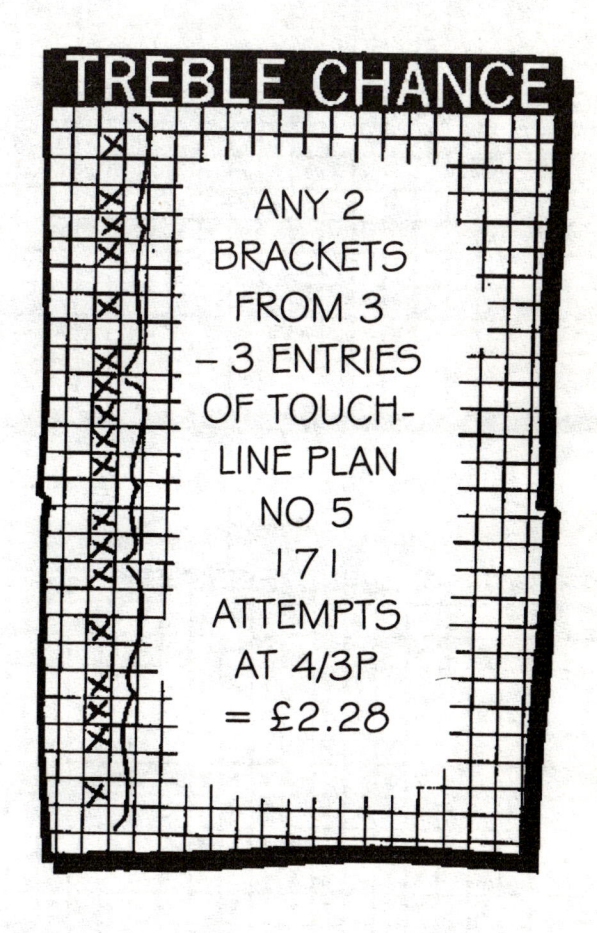

> **TREBLE CHANCE**
>
> ANY 2 BRACKETS FROM 3 – 3 ENTRIES OF TOUCHLINE PLAN NO 5
>
> 171 ATTEMPTS AT 4/3P = £2.28

This is an entry for a Littlewoods coupon at 4/3p per line.
The cost on Vernons would be 171 x 5/11p = £0.78
On Zetters it would cost 171 x 1/9p = £0.19

Touchline Plan No. 5 Checking Chart (part 1)

Results	1	2	3	4	5	6	7	8	9	10	11	12	13	14	15	16	17	18	19
	x	x	x	x	x	x	x	x	x	x	x	x	x	x	x	x	x	x	x
	x	x	x	x	x	x	x	x	x	x	x	x	x	x	x	x	x	x	x
	x	x	x	x	x	x	x	x	x	x	x	x	x	x					
	x	x	x	x	x	x	x	x	x							x	x	x	x
	x	x	x	x	x	x				x	x	x				x	x	x	
	x	x	x	x	x	x							x	x	x				x
	x	x					x	x		x	x		x	x		x	x		x
	x		x				x		x	x		x	x	x		x	x		x
		x	x				x		x	x	x		x		x	x		x	
				x	x		x	x			x	x		x	x		x	x	x
				x		x		x	x	x		x		x	x		x	x	
				x	x		x	x		x	x	x		x	x		x	x	
Points																			

Touchline Plan No. 5 Checking Chart (part 2)

Results	20	21	22	23	24	25	26	27	28	29	30	31	32	33	34	35	36	37	38
	x	x	x	x	x	x	x	x	x	x	x	x	x	x	x	x	x		
	x	x	x	x	x													x	x
						x	x	x	x	x	x	x	x	x				x	x
	x	x				x	x	x	x	x	x				x	x	x	x	x
			x	x	x	x	x	x				x	x	x	x	x	x	x	x
	x	x	x	x	x				x	x	x	x	x	x	x	x			
	x			x	x		x	x		x	x		x	x		x	x		x	x
		x	x			x	x		x	x		x	x		x	x		x	x	
	x	x		x	x		x	x	x	x			x	x	x		x		x
		x		x	x		x	x		x	x	x		x	x	x		x	
	x	x	x	x		x	x		x		x		x	x		x	x		x
	x		x		x	x		x		x	x	x	x			x	x	x	x
Points																			

Touchline Plan No. 5 Checking Chart
(part 3)

Results	39	40	41	42	43	44	45	46	47	48	49	50	51	52	53	54	55	56	57
														x	x				
		x	x	x	x	x	x	x	x	x				x		x			
		x	x	x	x	x	x				x	x	x		x	x			
		x	x	x	x			x	x	x	x	x	x				x	x	
		x				x	x	x	x	x	x	x	x	x			x		x
			x	x	x	x	x	x	x	x	x	x	x					x	x
			x	x			x	x		x		x		x	x	x	x	x	x
		x	x			x	x			x	x	x		x	x	x	x	x	x
		x			x	x	x		x	x		x		x	x	x	x	x	x
		x			x	x	x	x			x	x		x	x	x	x	x	x
		x	x	x			x	x	x		x			x	x	x	x	x	x
			x		x		x	x		x	x	x		x	x	x	x	x	x
Points																			

Pools Trivia

Many pools winners can't believe their luck when they actually hit the jackpot. One Merseyside couple who, after checking their coupon, refused to believe they had hit the big time and spent two hours talking each other out of telephoning a claim. A couple of days later they realised their mistake when they were presented with a cheque for £303,343!

⒖ *touchline plan number 8*

This Little Plan Is A Winner

Touch-Line Plan No. 8 is a very interesting little plan for the Treble Chance pool. It has won many useful dividends in the past and it will continue to do so as long as anyone cares to use it.

It is simply a set of 27 separate attempts of eight selections, spread here over your own chosen twelve matches. If you get any eight correct score draws among them, you must win a dividend and it could be a top one.

No other plan of this size has a better guarantee than this. But 27 attempts will only cost you 36 pence even on Littlewoods' million-plus pound jackpot pool at one and a third pence a go.

So here is a fourfold version of this plan covering sixteen matches for £1.44 (or £1.23 on Vernons at 5/11ths of a penny or 45 pence on Zetters' at 1/6th of a penny a go).

Use Littlewoods' full coupon, not the short version. Put sixteen crosses all in the same column against your own favoured score draws. Bracket them up into groups of four crosses so that you have four brackets.

Copy the instructions alongside as shown in the diagram followed by the stakes according to the coupon you are using. You have now filled in four entries of this plan, so naturally you get four times the guarantee.

Here is a quick way to check your entry. First circle all correct score draws marked with a cross on your copy coupon and pick out your best three brackets.

List the twelve Treble Chance values for these three brackets down the side of the full plan on this page. All you have to do now is to count up the number of points you have scored with the eight crosses in each one of the 27 columns of the plan to see if any of them are winners.

Littlewoods normally pay dividends for all attempts that have scored 21 points or more.

Pools Trivia

In March 1979, a young South Wales woman filled in her first ever Pools coupon, staking just 45p. She didn't check her copy coupon on Saturday as she was celebrating her 20th birthday party. Nor did she check her entry with the Sunday papers as she was announcing her engagement to her boyfriend.

Touchline Plan No. 8: Entry Guide

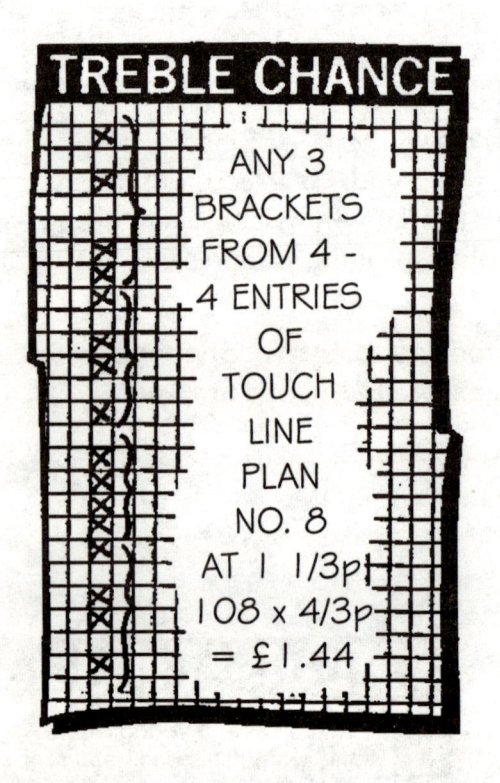

TREBLE CHANCE

ANY 3 BRACKETS FROM 4 - 4 ENTRIES OF TOUCH LINE PLAN NO. 8 AT 1 1/3p
108 x 4/3p = £1.44

This is an entry for a Littlewoods coupon at 4/3p per line.
The cost on Vernons would be 108 x 5/11p = £0.49
On Zetters it would cost 108 x1/9p = £0.12

Touchline Plan No. 8 Checking Chart

Results	1	2	3	4	5	6	7	8	9	10	11	12	13	14	15	16	17	18	19	20	21	22	23	24	25	26	27
	x	x	x	x	x	x	x	x	x	x	x	x	x	x	x	x	x	x									
	x	x	x	x	x	x	x	x	x	x	x	x	x							x	x	x	x				
	x	x	x	x	x	x	x							x	x	x	x		x	x	x	x	x	x	x	x	
	x	x	x	x					x	x				x	x	x		x	x	x	x	x		x	x	x	
	x				x	x		x	x		x			x	x		x	x	x	x		x		x	x		x
		x	x		x	x	x	x	x		x	x		x		x		x	x	x	x		x	x		x	x
		x	x				x	x		x	x		x	x	x	x	x	x	x	x	x	x	x	x		x	x
			x	x				x		x	x	x	x	x		x	x	x	x		x	x	x	x	x	x	x
				x	x	x	x	x	x	x	x	x	x		x		x	x		x		x	x	x	x	x	x
	x	x		x	x	x	x	x	x	x	x	x	x	x		x	x	x		x	x	x		x	x	x	x
		x																									
	x	x	x	x	x	x	x		x	x	x	x	x	x	x		x		x				x		x	x	x
	x	x	x	x	x	x	x		x	x	x	x	x		x	x		x				x	x				
Points																											

touchline plan number 20

A Plan Is The Answer

A full cover perm is simply a way of entering a greater number of crosses in a single column than the eight selections required for the Treble Chance pool and taking any eight from that number.

But a full cover perm is no use if you want to cover a large number of matches. For instance a full cover perm of any eight from your own chosen 32 matches would involve over ten million separate attempts!

The answer is to use a plan. You do not get a blanket cover from the games you have chosen but you do get a guarantee.

Here is how you enter Touch-Line Plan No. 20 on Zetters' coupon at 900 goes for a pound (or £10.45 on Littlewoods at 75 goes for a pound, or £3.56 on Vernons at 220 goes for a pound).

Choose 32 games you think could end in a score draw that scores the maximum of three Treble Chance points. Mark your first 16 selections with 16 crosses in one column and your remaining sixteen with 16 crosses in another column.

Copy the instructions alongside as shown in the diagram. You are now guaranteed at least six in a line (possibly seven or even eight) whenever you get any five correct score draws in each of your two columns. There are of course many other ways of winning.

If you think you could be a winner you check your entry like this. Write down the 32 Treble Chance values for the 32 crosses on your copy coupon. Transfer your first column of 16 values in correct order to the left-hand column of Checking Chart A on the page overleaf.

Do the same thing with your second column of 16 values using Checking Chart B.

Count up the total number of points you have scored with the four crosses in each column of both blocks. Write the totals at the bottom.

Finally circle the best total in each chart. Your best score will be the total of these two circled totals added together.

Pools Trivia

In February 1980, brewery worker Dave Preston, of Burton-On-Trent, scooped the first dividend jackpot on both Littlewoods and Vernons in the same week - netting a massive £953,874.10p!

Touchline Plan No. 20: Entry Guide

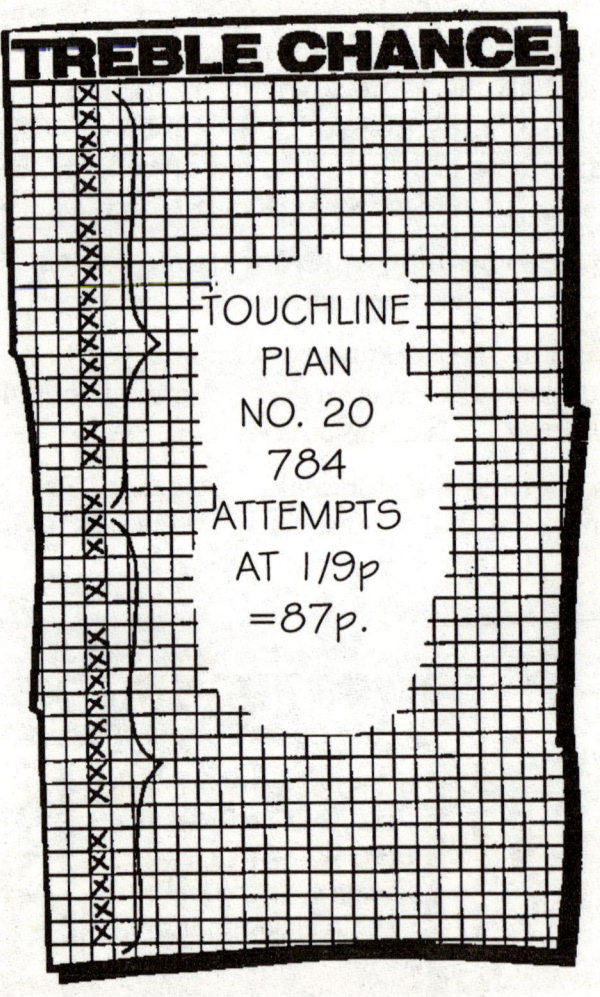

This is an entry for a Zetters coupon at 1/9p per line.
The cost on Vernons would be 784 x 5/11p = £3.56
On Littlewoods it would cost 784 x 4/3p = £10.45

Results	1	2	3	4	5	6	7	8	9	10	11	12	13	14	15	16	17	18	19	20	21	22	23	24	25	26	27	28
	×		×		×								×	×	×		×		×									
		×		×		×							×		×	×	×	×	×	×	×	×	×	×	×	×	×	
	×		×		×									×							×		×					
		×		×			×	×	×	×			×		×	×		×		×	×	×	×	×	×	×	×	×
	×						×	×	×								×	×	×					×	×	×	×	
		×	×				×	×				×	×			×		×			×				×	×		
				×				×	×	×	×	×		×	×	×		×	×	×		×		×				
			×	×							×	×				×				×		×	×	×	×	×	×	×
					×	×			×	×	×		×				×		×	×	×		×					
						×	×	×		×	×	×	×		×				×		×	×	×	×				
					×					×	×	×		×				×			×	×	×	×				×
Points																													

Touchline Plan No. 20 Checking Chart A

Results	1	2	3	4	5	6	7	8	9	10	11	12	13	14	15	16	17	18	19	20	21	22	23	24	25	26	27	28
	X		X		X										X	X												X
		X		X									X		X			X				X	X		X			
		X			X													X				X			X				
		X	X										X						X					X						
X		X										X		X				X						X					
			X	X				X			X							X		X								
					X	X				X		X									X									
	X					X	X				X				X					X				X				
						X	X	X					X				X												
							X		X	X								X					X							
X										X	X									X		X					X		
										X	X	X							X							X			
					X						X	X	X								X				X				X
		X	X										X	X											X				
				X				X					X	X								X			X			
	X														X	X				X								
X															X	X									X	X	
					X		X					X					X	X									
X																	X	X				X						X
									X					X			X	X									
									X	X									X	X	X					X		
						X					X	X				X				X	X	X					
				X								X	X					X			X	X	X			
	X			X								X	X	X						X	X	X
Points																													

Touchline Plan No. 20 Checking Chart B

touchline plan number 23

Plans That Spread The Dividends

Full cover perms are a very popular way of going in for the Treble Chance pool. But they have the disadvantage of bunching the minor dividends in with the top one, so that in the long run you do not win so often.

Plans have been devised by the pool companies and the newspapers that spread the dividends so that they arrive one or two at a time. So by using a plan you are likely to win more often.

My Touch-Line plans are specially designed to be small in size and easy to check. This idea uses Touch-Line Plan No. 23 five times on Zetters' coupon to cover twenty matches at a total cost of exactly one pound at their bonus stake of six goes a penny (£2.75 on Vernons at 220 goes for a pound or eight pounds on Littlewoods at 1-1/3rd pence a go).

Put twenty crosses all in the same column against the twenty games you have picked out for yourself as being likely to end as score draws that have the maximum value of three Treble Chance points.

Bracket them up into groups of four crosses so that you have five brackets.

Copy the instructions alongside as shown but amend the stakes if necessary to suit the coupon you are using.

The guarantee that goes with this entry is that if you get any ten score draws in any four of your five brackets, you will win four dividends and one of them could with luck be a top one. There are of course many other ways of winning with as few as five score draws.

Checking is quick and easy. First circle all crosses on your copy coupon that have captured three points for a score draw and pick out your best four brackets.

List the sixteen Treble Chance values for these four brackets in the same order down the side of all four sections of the full plan on this page.

You can now count up the total number of points you have scored with the eight crosses in each one of the 120 columns of the plan to see if any of them are winners.

Touchline Plan No. 23: Entry Guide

TREBLE CHANCE

ANY 4 BRACKETS FROM 5 - 5 ENTRIES OF TOUCHLINE PLAN NO. 23 AT 1/6p. 5 x 20p = £1.00.

This is an entry for a Zetters coupon at 1/6p per line.
The cost on Vernons would be 600 x 5/11p = £2.73
On Littlewoods it would cost 600 x4/3p = £8.00

Touchline Plan No. 23 Checking Chart part 1

Results	1	2	3	4	5	6	7	8	9	10	11	12	13	14	15	16	17	18	19	20	21	22	23	24	25	26	27	28	29	30
	x	x	x	x	x	x	x									x	x	x	x	x	x	x								
	x	x	x	x	x	x	x																x	x	x	x	x	x	x	x
	x	x	x					x	x	x	x			x	x	x	x					x	x	x	x					
	x	x	x					x	x	x	x							x	x	x	x					x	x	x	x	x
	x			x	x			x	x			x	x			x	x			x	x			x	x			x	x	
	x			x	x			x	x			x	x					x	x			x	x			x	x			x
		x		x		x		x		x		x		x	x		x		x		x		x		x		x		x	
		x		x		x		x		x		x		x		x		x		x		x		x		x		x		x
	x			x	x			x	x	x	x			x	x			x	x			x	x	x	x					
	x			x	x			x	x	x	x					x	x	x	x			x	x						x	x
		x			x		x		x		x		x	x		x		x		x		x		x		x	x		x	
		x			x		x		x		x		x		x		x		x		x	x		x		x			x	x
			x	x			x		x	x			x	x	x			x	x			x	x	x				x	x	
			x	x			x		x	x						x	x			x	x			x	x			x	x	x
			x		x	x		x		x	x	x			x		x	x	x		x		x				x	x		
			x		x	x		x		x	x			x	x			x	x	x		x			x	x	x			x
Points																														

Touchline Plan No. 23 Checking Chart part 2

Results	31	32	33	34	35	36	37	38	39	40	41	42	43	44	45	46	47	48	49	50	51	52	53	54	55	56	57	58	59	60
	x	x			x		x	x	x	x		x		x			x		x		x	x	x	x						
	x	x				x	x	x	x	x		x		x		x		x		x						x	x	x	x	
			x	x		x	x	x			x	x	x		x			x		x	x		x	x		x	x			
			x	x		x	x	x			x	x		x		x		x		x		x	x			x	x		x	x
	x		x			x	x		x		x		x	x	x	x	x			x		x		x		x				
	x		x		x		x		x		x	x	x	x			x		x		x		x		x					x
	x	x				x				x	x	x		x	x	x		x		x	x	x	x			x	x	x		
	x	x			x		x			x	x		x	x		x		x	x	x	x	x								
		x		x	x		x	x		x		x	x		x	x			x	x	x			x				x		x
		x		x	x	x			x		x	x	x		x		x		x		x			x		x		x	x	
			x	x		x			x	x			x	x		x	x	x		x	x	x			x	x			x	x
			x	x		x			x	x		x	x		x	x		x	x	x			x	x			x	x	
		x		x	x		x	x	x				x	x		x		x	x			x	x		x		x	x		x
		x		x	x	x		x	x		x		x			x	x		x	x		x	x	x		x				x
	x		x		x		x		x				x		x	x	x	x	x		x		x		x		x		x	
	x		x		x			x		x					x	x	x	x	x		x		x		x			x		
Points																														

Touchline Plan No. 23 Checking Chart part 3

Results	61	62	63	64	65	66	67	68	69	70	71	72	73	74	75	76	77	78	79	80	81	82	83	84	85	86	87	88	89	90
	x	x	x			x		x	x		x			x				x	x	x	x		x						x	x
	x	x	x	x				x			x	x		x			x	x	x	x	x		x			x				x
	x			x	x	x			x	x	x	x			x		x			x	x		x			x	x			
	x			x	x	x			x	x	x		x	x					x	x			x	x				x	x	
	x	x	x	x					x		x	x	x		x				x	x			x			x	x	x		
		x		x		x		x		x	x			x	x	x		x		x		x	x		x	x	x		x	
			x		x		x	x		x	x			x	x			x			x	x			x	x		x		
			x		x		x	x	x	x	x		x		x	x			x			x		x	x		x			x
	x			x	x	x				x	x		x	x		x	x		x	x	x		x	x	x		x			
	x	x	x			x		x		x		x		x						x	x	x	x	x		x				x
	x			x	x	x		x				x		x	x				x	x		x	x			x	x		x	x
		x			x	x	x			x		x	x			x			x	x		x	x	x			x	x	x	
			x	x	x		x	x			x			x	x		x		x	x			x	x	x		x	x		
			x	x	x			x			x			x		x	x			x	x		x	x		x	x		x	
		x			x	x	x			x	x		x		x	x	x	x			x			x			x	x	x	x

Points

Touchline Plan No. 23 Checking Chart part 4

Results	91	92	93	94	95	96	97	98	99	100	101	102	103	104	105	106	107	108	109	110	111	112	113	114	115	116	117	118	119	120
	x	x			x	x	x	x		x				x		x		x	x				x	x		x		x		
	x	x				x	x	x	x	x		x		x					x	x	x			x		x		x		x
			x	x	x	x			x	x	x	x	x	x			x		x			x		x		x				x
	x			x		x			x	x	x	x	x			x	x		x				x		x			x	x	
	x			x			x	x		x			x	x	x	x	x		x			x		x	x					x
	x			x		x	x		x				x	x	x		x		x	x		x		x			x	x		
		x		x	x		x		x			x	x	x		x	x	x						x	x			x		
	x	x					x	x	x	x		x		x	x	x	x	x						x		x		x		x
		x		x	x		x		x			x	x		x		x	x	x		x	x					x			x
		x		x		x		x	x	x		x		x	x			x	x	x		x	x		x	x		x		
			x	x	x	x				x	x		x		x			x	x		x	x		x		x		x	x	
			x	x			x	x	x		x				x	x	x	x	x		x		x		x			x		x
	x	x						x	x	x	x		x		x			x	x	x	x	x	x		x		x			
	x		x		x		x			x		x			x	x	x		x	x	x		x	x						x
		x		x		x		x			x	x		x	x	x		x			x	x	x			x		x		x
			x	x			x	x		x	x			x			x			x		x		x		x		x	x	

Points

touchline plan number 26

A Plan For All Seasons

You can now have no fewer than 2,700 goes at nine goes a penny on Zetters' low stake Treble Chance pool for an outlay of three pounds a week, not only this week but also every week throughout the year. Here is one way of doing it.

Remember that all scoring draws, including the higher scoring draws (2-2, 3-3 etc), now score the maximum of three Treble Chance points.

Put 20 crosses, all in the same column against 20 possible scoring draws. Bracket them up into ten pairs. Copy the instructions alongside following the example shown in the diagram.

You have now filled in 45 entries of Touch-Line Plan No. 26. In its basic form, this plan is made up of sixty single attempts of eight crosses.

If you get any eight score draws in any eight of your ten pairs, you will have either one dividend winning column that includes at least seven of them or else you will have three columns that include six of them.

Any of these three columns could be a winner depending on the results of the other two matches in that column.

To check your entry you must first pick out your best eight brackets. You can easily do this by circling all correct score draws marked with a cross on your copy coupon.

List the sixteen Treble Chance values for these best eight brackets down the side of both sections of the full plan on pages 69 ad 70.

You can now count up the total number of points you have scored with the eight crosses in each one of the sixty columns of the plan to see if any of them are winners, usually 21 points or more.

This plan can also be entered on Vernon's coupon for £12.27 at 5/11ths of a penny a go. On Littlewoods at 1-1/3rd pence a go it will cost you a total of £36.00.

Pools Trivia

A Pools win often brings much needed financial relief - especially if like Martin Smith you have been on strike for 11 weeks. During the 1984 pit strike, the Doncaster miner, his father and brother shared a £602,708 jackpot in the week he had decided he could no longer afford his weekly contribution to the family entry.

Touchline Plan No. 26: Entry Guide

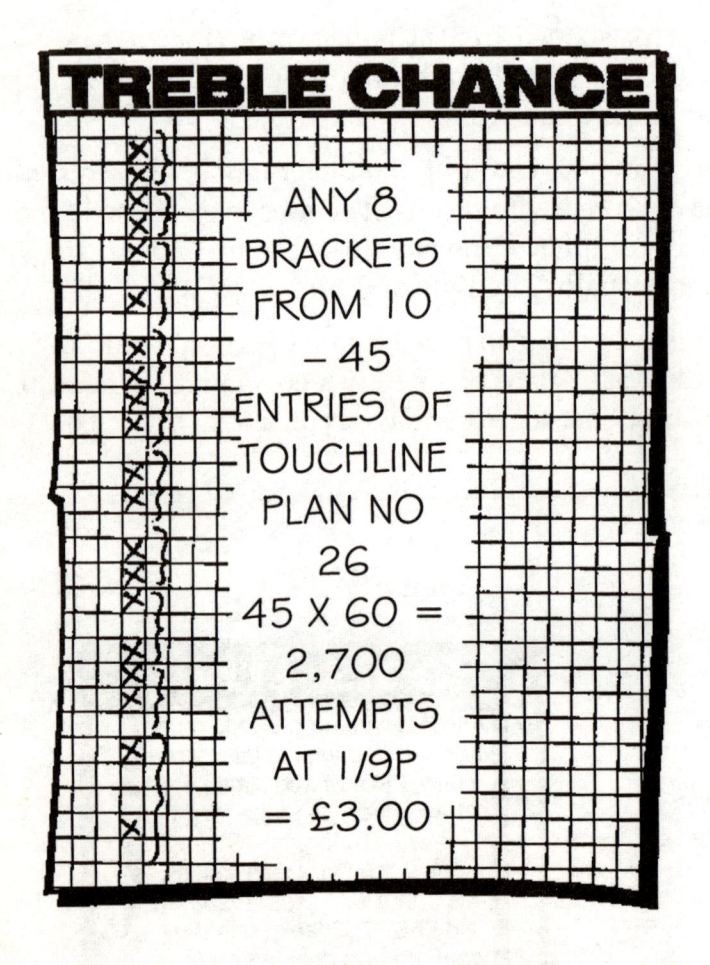

> **TREBLE CHANCE**
>
> ANY 8 BRACKETS FROM 10 – 45 ENTRIES OF TOUCHLINE PLAN NO 26
>
> 45 X 60 = 2,700 ATTEMPTS AT 1/9P = £3.00

This is an entry for a Zetters coupon at 1/9p per line.
The cost on Vernons would be 2,700 x 5/11p = £12.27
On Zetters it would cost 2,700 x 4/3p = £36.00

Results	1	2	3	4	5	6	7	8	9	10	11	12	13	14	15	16	17	18	19	20	21	22	23	24	25	26	27	28	29	30
	x	x	x	x	x	x	x															x								
	x	x	x	x	x	x	x	x	x																					
	x	x	x					x	x	x	x					x	x		x				x	x	x	x	x	x	x	x
	x	x		x	x			x	x	x	x				x			x	x	x		x	x	x	x		x	x	x	x
	x			x	x	x		x	x	x	x	x				x			x	x	x			x		x	x			x
	x							x	x	x	x	x	x		x		x				x	x	x		x	x		x	x	x
		x	x			x	x	x		x	x	x	x	x		x	x	x			x	x		x	x	x	x	x		
		x	x	x		x	x				x	x	x	x	x	x		x	x	x		x			x	x	x	x	x	x
	x	x			x	x	x					x	x	x	x		x		x	x	x		x	x		x			x	x
				x	x		x	x	x				x	x	x	x	x	x	x	x		x	x	x	x	x	x	x	x	x
	x	x		x	x	x	x	x	x	x				x				x	x	x		x	x	x		x	x	x	x	x
		x	x	x	x	x	x		x	x	x				x	x	x	x	x	x	x		x	x	x	x	x	x	x	
			x	x					x	x	x	x	x	x	x		x		x	x	x	x	x						x	x
			x	x	x	x		x	x				x	x	x	x	x	x		x	x	x	x	x	x	x	x	x	x	x
			x	x	x	x	x	x	x	x	x				x	x		x				x	x	x			x		x	
Points																														

Touchline Plan No. 26 Checking Chart part 1

Results	31	32	33	34	35	36	37	38	39	40	41	42	43	44	45	46	47	48	49	50	51	52	53	54	55	56	57	58	59	60
	×	×	×	×								×	×	×	×			×	×			×		×		×	×	×		
				×	×	×	×	×			×				×			×	×				×		×	×	×		×	×
					×		×		×	×	×		×	×		×	×	×				×			×		×	×		×
	×	×	×				×	×	×	×		×			×	×	×	×		×			×		×		×		×	
	×	×		×	×		×	×	×						×	×					×			×	×		×	×	×	×
	×		×			×		×		×	×	×		×	×				×	×	×	×		×		×	×	×	×	×
	×	×			×	×	×				×		×		×	×				×	×				×	×			×	
			×					×	×	×	×	×	×	×					×	×	×	×	×			×	×	×	×	×
		×	×				×	×	×		×	×	×		×		×		×	×	×	×			×	×		×	×	
	×	×	×	×		×	×	×						×			×		×	×	×	×	×					×	×	×
	×	×		×	×	×	×		×	×		×	×	×			×	×					×				×			×
			×	×	×	×		×	×		×		×	×	×	×	×			×		×	×	×	×	×	×			×
		×		×		×	×	×	×		×			×	×			×		×	×	×	×	×		×				×
			×						×	×	×	×	×			×		×												
Points																														

Touchline Plan No. 26 Checking Chart part 2

19 *touchline plan number 27*

Touch-Line Plans Are Different

Most newspaper plans for the Treble Chance pool are made up of a large number of single eight-match attempts spread over a fixed number of games that you choose for yourself.

The big drawback is that the checking process is very laborious and it takes a long time. Touch-Line Plans are different. They are small plans used in multiple form. To arrive at the number of points you have scored with the best attempt you have sent in, you only have a small plan to check.

Touch-Line plans can be sculptured to cover any number of matches. Stakes can be big or small and you can use any one of the popular pools coupons.

This version, for example, uses Touch-line plan No. 27 four times to cover a massive 32 matches on Vernons coupon for a weekly outlay of £14.32 at 75 goes for a pound (or £3.50 on Zetters at 900 goes for a pound or £42.00 on Littlewoods at 75 goes for a pound.)

To use it you put 32 crosses in one column against your own choice of 32 possible score draws and put a bracket round each group of four crosses so that you have eight brackets.

Copy they instructions alongside as shown in the diagram and your entry is complete. If you get any eight correct score draws in any four of your eight brackets you must have either one attempt that includes at least seven of them or two attempts that include at least six of them.

There are of course many other ways of winning top or minor dividends.

You usually need at least four correct score draws to be in with a chance. If you think you are, you should circle all crosses on your copy coupon that have scored three Treble Chance points for a score draw and pick out your best four brackets.

List the sixteen Treble Chance scores for these four brackets down the side of the full plan on the following pages. You can now count up how many points your have scored with the eight crosses in each one of the 42 columns of the plan to find out if any of them are likely to have won anything.

Touchline Plan No. 27: Entry Guide

8 MATCH TREBLE CHANCE

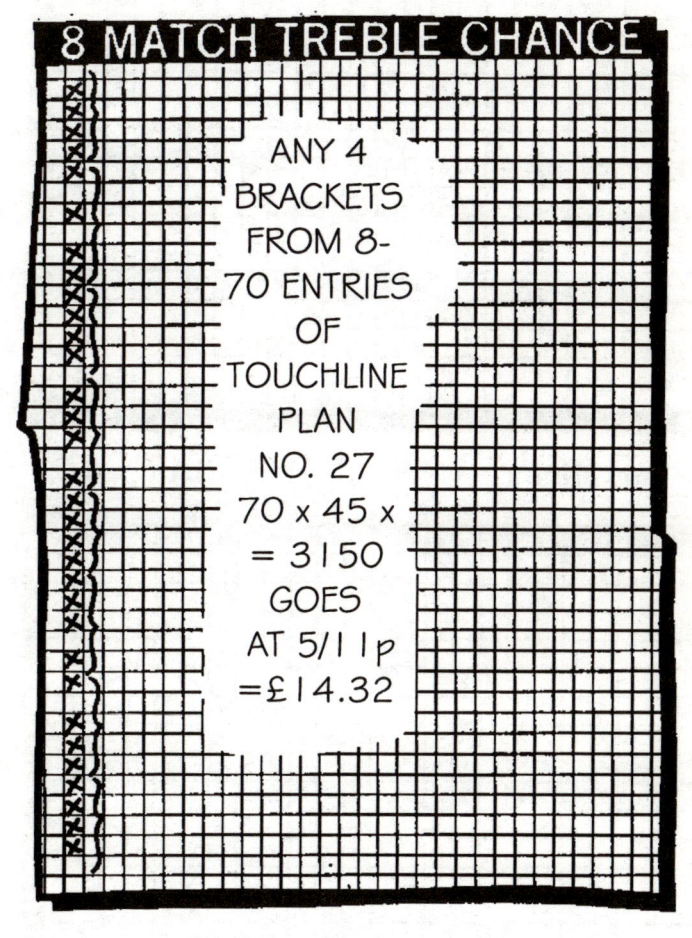

ANY 4 BRACKETS FROM 8-70 ENTRIES OF TOUCHLINE PLAN NO. 27
70 x 45 x = 3150
GOES AT 5/11p
= £14.32

This is an entry for a Versnons coupon at 5/11p per line.
The cost on Littlewoods would be 3150 x 4/3p = £42.00
On Zetters it would cost 3150 x 1/9p = £3.50

Touchline Plan No. 8 Checking Chart part 1

Results	1	2	3	4	5	6	7	8	9	10	11	12	13	14	15	16	17	18	19	20	21
	X	X	X	X	X	X	X	X	X	X	X	X	X	X	X	X	X	X	X	X	X
	X	X	X	X	X	X	X	X	X	X	X										
	X	X	X									X	X	X	X	X	X				
	X	X	X															X	X	X	X
	X			X	X	X	X				X	X	X					X	X	X	X
	X			X	X	X		X							X	X	X	X			
	X					X		X	X	X	X	X	X		X				X		
	X						X	X	X	X			X		X	X				X	X
		X		X	X			X	X		X				X		X		X		
		X		X	X			X	X			X	X	X		X			X		X
		X				X	X	X			X	X				X			X		X
		X				X	X	X		X		X	X	X		X	X		X		
			X	X			X		X		X	X		X		X	X				
			X	X			X	X		X		X		X		X	X				X
			X		X	X	X			X		X				X		X			X
			X		X	X		X		X			X	X		X				X	X
Points																					

Touchline Plan No. 8 Checking Chart part 2

Results	22	23	24	25	26	27	28	29	30	31	32	33	34	35	36	37	38	39	40	41	42
	X	X	X	X																	
					X	X	X	X	X	X	X	X	X	X							
					X	X	X	X	X	X					X	X	X	X			
	X	X	X	X						X	X	X	X	X	X	X	X	X			
					X	X	X			X	X		X	X			X	X			
	X	X	X		X			X	X			X	X	X	X			X	X		
	X	X		X			X	X	X	X	X					X	X	X	X		
			X	X		X	X			X			X	X		X	X	X	X		
	X			X		X		X			X		X		X		X		X		X
		X	X		X		X		X	X		X		X	X		X		X		X
		X	X		X		X		X	X	X		X			X		X	X		X
	X			X		X		X			X		X		X		X	X			X
		X	X		X		X	X			X	X		X	X				X	X
	X				X	X			X		X			X		X	X			X	X
	X		X	X		X			X	X	X	X			X			X		X	X
		X		X			X	X		X	X			X	X			X		X	X
Points																					

20 *touchline plan number 28*

Save Money On The Pools

Many people have won big money on the pools by picking purely random numbers. That may be so, but it doesn't alter the fact that by using your skill with the help of statistical information you can certainly multiply your chances.

The Treble Chance pool is your gateway to the big money. A plan has advantages over a full cover perm because a plan spreads your efforts over far more matches to give you a better chance of trapping the eight score draws (1-1, 2-2 etc.) needed to capture the smaller dividends – or even a top one that could run into millions.

Touch-Line plans are small and easy to check and they can be used in multiple form to suit all pockets and purses. This example is a sixfold version of Touch-Line Plan No. 28 that covers 28 matches on Littlewoods' coupon for £2.88, very different from a full cover perm of any 8 from 28 that would run into over three million attempts.

You can save even more money by using Vernons' coupon where it will cost you 98 pence at 5/11ths of a penny a go or on Zetters, 36 pence at six goes a penny.

Pick your own 28 most likely score draws. Identify them on the coupon by putting 28 crosses all in the same column. Bracket them into groups of seven crosses so that you have four brackets. Complete your entry by copying the instructions and stakes alongside as shown in the diagram.

The merit of this arrangement is that any nine score draws in any two brackets will win you at least a minor dividend and possibly a top one.

The first checking step is to circle all correct score draws on your copy coupon so that you can pick out your best two brackets.

Mark up the fourteen Treble Chance values for these two brackets. If you have four or more it is worth a full check. Transfer the fourteen values to the blank column on the left of the full plan on this page.

You could be a winner if the total score for the eight crosses in any one column comes to 21 points or more.

Touchline Plan No. 28: Entry Guide

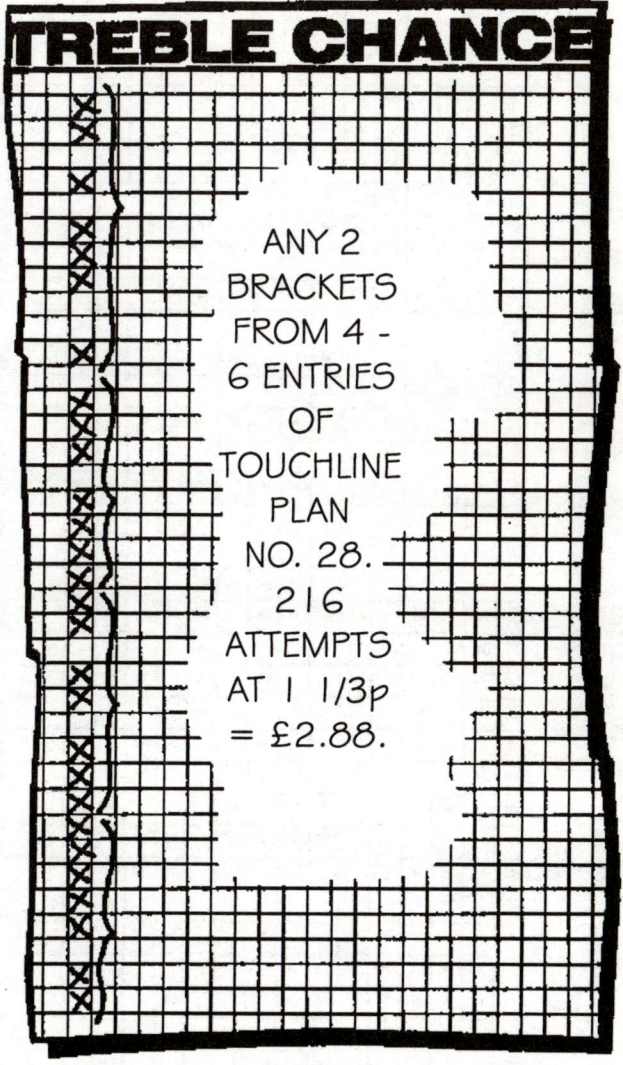

TREBLE CHANCE

ANY 2 BRACKETS FROM 4 - 6 ENTRIES OF TOUCHLINE PLAN NO. 28. 216 ATTEMPTS AT 1 1/3p = £2.88.

This is an entry for a Littlewoods coupon at 4/3p per line.
The cost on Vernons would be 216 x 5/11p = £0.98
On Zetters it would cost 216 x 1/9p = £0.36

Touchline Plan No. 28 Checking Chart

Results	1	2	3	4	5	6	7	8	9	10	11	12	13	14	15	16	17	18	19	20	21	22	23	24	25	26	27	28	29	30	31	32	33	34	35	36
	×	×	×	×	×	×	×	×	×	×	×	×	×	×	×	×	×	×	×	×											×					
	×	×	×	×	×	×	×	×	×	×				×							×	×	×	×	×	×	×	×	×	×	×	×	×	×	×	
		×	×	×	×	×					×	×	×		×	×	×	×	×	×	×	×	×	×	×	×	×	×	×	×	×	×	×	×	×	
		×	×					×	×	×		×	×	×	×	×	×	×	×	×					×							×	×	×	×	×
	×	×			×		×	×	×	×	×		×			×					×	×	×	×	×						×	×	×	×	×	×
	×	×				×	×	×	×	×	×	×		×	×		×	×	×	×	×	×	×	×		×	×	×	×	×	×	×	×			×
		×	×	×	×	×	×	×	×	×	×	×	×	×		×		×	×	×	×		×	×	×	×	×	×	×	×	×					×
Points																																				

21 *touchline plan number 29*

This Is A Better Way

There are several reasons why the pools are more attractive than the National Lottery. To begin with, the prizes are more evenly distributed so you are much more likely to win the pools than you are to win the Lottery.

Furthermore, no claims are required. If you are a winner, your winnings will drop through your letter box within a few days.

In addition you have more control over your own destiny. You can choose a system of entry such as a full cover perm that brings you a bunch of minor dividends along with the big one.

Or you can use a plan that spreads out your dividends to give you more winning weeks. I think this is a better way, so here is a suggested system of entry.

It uses Touch-Line Plan No. 29 ten times over to cover 25 matches of your own choice for a total weekly outlay of £3.50 on Vernons' coupon at 5/11ths of a penny a go (£10.27 on Littlewoods at 1-1/3rd pence a go or 86 pence on Zetters at nine goes a penny).

Put 25 Crosses in one of the right-hand Treble Chance columns against the 25 matches you prefer. Bracket them up into groups of five crosses so that you have five brackets.

Copy the instructions alongside as shown in the example on this page. That is all you have to do.

You have now filled in 770 separate attempts to win a dividend. If you get any nine score draws in any three of your five brackets, you must win at least one dividend. If you get any eleven score draws in any three brackets it must be a top dividend. There are also many other ways of winning with as few as five score draws.

If you could be a winner, you should first circle all correct score draws on your copy coupon and pick out your best three brackets. Now refer to the Treble Chance check published over the weekend and list the fifteen Treble Chance scores for these three brackets in correct coupon order down the side of all three sections of the full plan on this page.

You can now count up the total number of points you have scored with the eight crosses in each one of the 77 columns of the plan to find out if any of them are winners.

Touchline Plan No. 29: Entry Guide

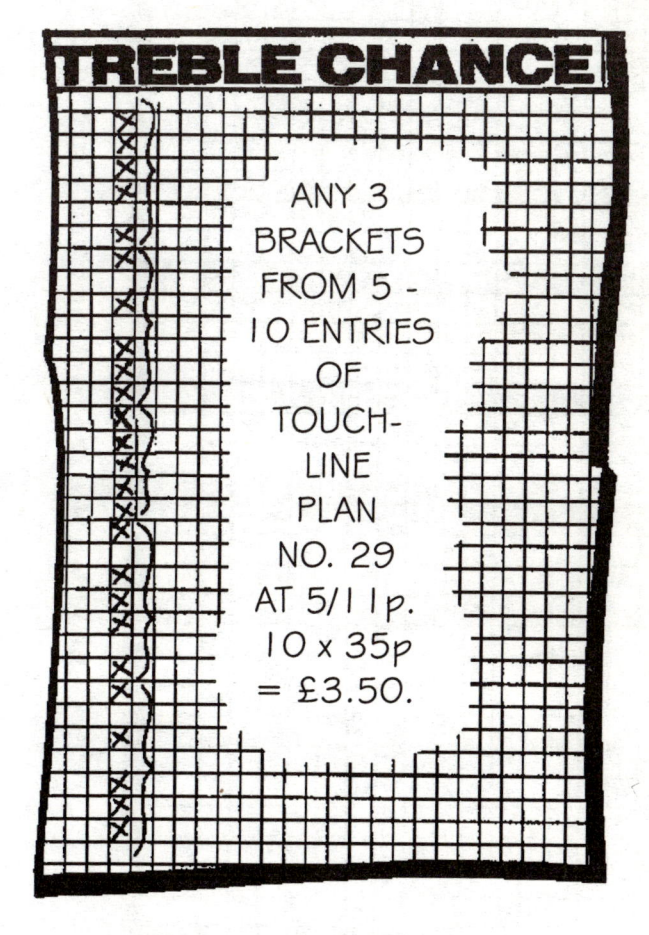

TREBLE CHANCE

ANY 3 BRACKETS FROM 5 - 10 ENTRIES OF TOUCH-LINE PLAN NO. 29 AT 5/11p.
10 x 35p = £3.50.

This is an entry for a Vernons coupon at 5/11p per line.
The cost on Littlewoods would be 770 x 4/3p = £10.27
On Zetters it would cost 770 x1/9p = £0.86

Touchline Plan No. 29 Checking Chart part 1

Results	1	2	3	4	5	6	7	8	9	10	11	12	13	14	15	16	17	18	19	20	21	22	23	24	25	26	27	28	29	30	31	32	33	34	35	36	37	38
	x	x	x	x	x	x	x	x	x	x	x	x	x	x	x	x	x	x	x	x	x	x	x	x	x	x	x	x	x	x	x	x	x	x	x	x	x	x
		x	x	x	x	x	x	x	x	x	x	x	x	x	x	x	x	x	x	x	x	x	x	x	x	x	x	x	x									
	x	x	x	x	x	x	x	x	x	x															x	x	x	x	x	x	x							
	x	x	x	x	x	x	x			x	x	x	x	x	x	x		x						x	x		x	x	x		x			x	x	x	x	x
		x			x	x	x	x		x	x	x	x	x	x	x			x												x	x	x		x	x	x	x
			x		x	x		x	x		x										x	x	x		x	x	x	x	x	x	x	x	x					
							x	x	x							x		x		x	x										x	x		x				
	x											x		x	x	x	x		x	x	x	x	x	x	x		x	x	x	x	x	x	x	x	x	x	x	x
					x	x	x		x	x	x				x	x	x		x	x	x	x	x	x				x	x		x	x		x	x	x	x	x
		x	x	x	x		x	x	x	x	x		x	x	x	x	x	x	x	x	x	x		x		x	x	x	x	x	x	x					x	x
						x						x		x				x	x	x			x				x				x	x	x	x	x			x
						x	x	x	x	x			x		x	x	x		x	x	x			x	x	x		x	x	x			x	x	x	x	x	
										x												x																

Results

Results	39	40	41	42	43	44	45	46	47	48	49	50	51	52	53	54	55	56	57	58	59	60	61	62	63	64	65	66	67	68	69	70	71	72	73	74	75	76	77
	×	×	×																					×										×						
	×	×																					×		×				×										
																																		×					
				×	×															×	×	×	×		×	×	×	×	×	×	×	×	×	×	×	×	×	×	×
	×	×	×	×	×	×	×							×	×	×	×	×	×		×		×	×	×	×	×					×		×	×	×	×	×	
	×	×	×	×	×	×	×	×	×	×		×	×	×		×	×	×	×	×	×	×	×	×	×	×	×			×	×	×	×	×	×	×	×	×	
			×	×	×	×	×	×	×			×				×	×	×	×	×	×	×		×	×			×	×	×	×	×		×	×	×	×	×	
				×	×	×			×	×	×	×		×	×	×	×	×	×		×	×	×	×	×	×	×	×	×	×	×	×	×	×	×	×	×	×	
	×	×	×			×					×		×	×		×	×	×		×			×	×		×		×	×	×	×	×	×	×	×	×	×	×	
	×	×	×	×	×						×	×	×	×	×	×	×	×	×		×		×	×	×	×	×	×	×	×	×	×	×	×	×	×	×	×	
				×					×					×	×	×	×	×		×	×		×	×	×	×			×	×	×	×	×	×					
			×			×	×		×	×			×	×	×	×	×	×		×	×				×	×	×	×	×			×		×		×	×			
	×	×	×	×	×	×	×	×	×	×	×	×	×	×	×	×	×	×	×	×	×	×	×	×	×	×	×	×	×	×	×	×	×	×	×	×	×	×	
	×	×	×	×	×	×		×	×	×				×	×		×	×	×	×	×	×	×			×		×	×										
Results																																							

Touchline Plan No. 29 Checking Chart part 2

touchline plan number 30

This Pool Plan Is Simple

One of the great beauties of the series of Touch-Line plans for the Treble Chance pool is their simplicity.

With a big plan you have to check hundreds of attempts one at a time. Instead, you use a little plan many times over. Then by picking out the best one of these plan entries you only need to check just a few columns.

Touch-Line Plan No. 30 is a set of 36 single attempts spread over twelve matches. If you get any three top scoring draws in the top six, plus another three in the bottom six, one of the 36 attempts will include all six of them.

Here is a way of using this plan ten times to cover thirty matches at a cost of £4.80 on Littlewoods' coupon at 1-1/3rd pence for each attempt; (£1.64 on Vernons at 5/11ths of a penny, or on Zetters either 60 pence at six goes a penny or 40 pence at nine goes a penny).

Most games listed on the coupon have around a 13 per cent chance of ending as a one-all jackpot draw. So you have a wide choice.

Put 30 crosses in a single column to the right of the matches, and bracket them up into groups of six crosses so that you have five brackets.

Copy the instructions alongside as shown to complete your entry. You are now guaranteed all six together whenever you get any three top scoring draws in any two of your five brackets.

Checking is simple. First circle all crosses on your copy coupon which have captured three points for a jackpot draw. Pick out your best two brackets. List the twelve Treble Chance values for these two brackets in the same order down the side of the full plan on this page.

You now have only 36 columns to check to find out whether or not your are likely to have won anything.

Pools Trivia

David Horobin scooped £901,185 in July 1985 on the Australian Pools - a record at the time - but refused to close his dry cleaning shop to go to London for a presentation. Instead he was at the shop early in the morning to make sure garments due for collection that day were ready, and the presentation was actually held at the counter between serving customers!

Touchline Plan No. 30: Entry Guide

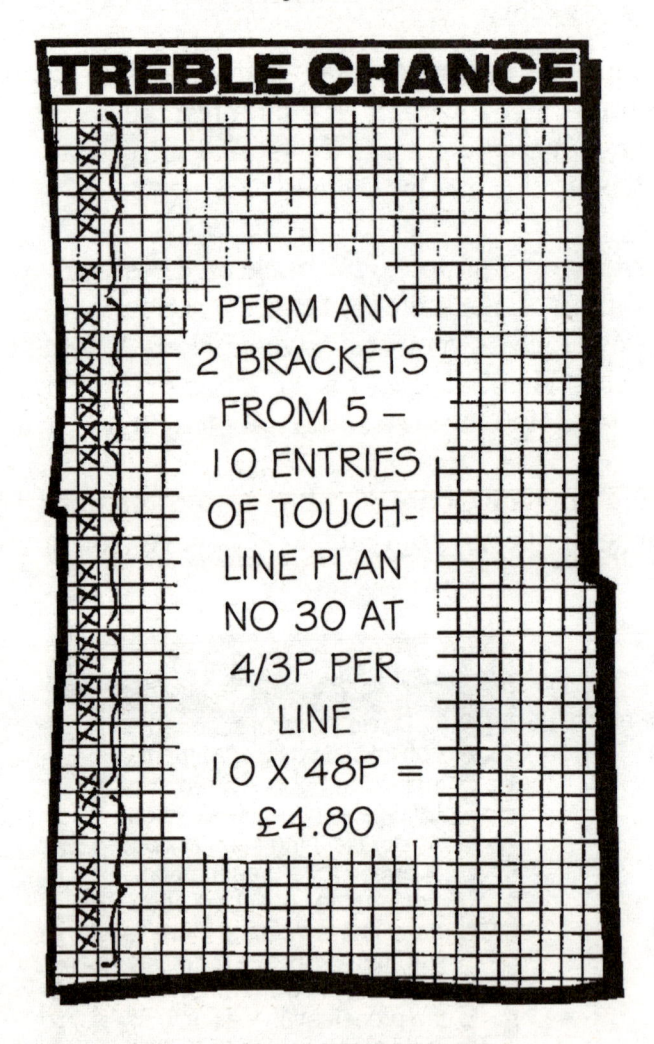

> **TREBLE CHANCE**
>
> PERM ANY 2 BRACKETS FROM 5 – 10 ENTRIES OF TOUCHLINE PLAN NO 30 AT 4/3P PER LINE
>
> 10 X 48P = £4.80

This is an entry for a Littlewoods coupon at 4/3p per line.
The cost on Vernons would be 360 x 5/11p = £1.64
On Zetters it would cost 360 x 1/6p = £0.60; or £0.40 at 1/9p

Touchline Plan No. 30 Checking Chart

Results	1	2	3	4	5	6	7	8	9	10	11	12	13	14	15	16	17	18	19	20	21	22	23	24	25	26	27	28	29	30	31	32	33	34	35	36
	x	x	x	x	x	x	x	x	x	x	x	x	x	x	x	x	x	x																		
	x	x	x	x	x	x	x	x	x	x	x	x	x	x	x	x	x	x							x	x	x	x	x	x	x	x	x	x	x	
	x	x	x	x	x	x	x	x	x	x	x	x	x	x	x	x	x	x	x	x	x	x	x	x	x	x	x	x	x	x	x	x	x	x	x	x
				x			x	x		x	x							x	x	x	x	x	x	x												
			x		x	x		x	x	x		x							x	x	x	x	x	x	x	x	x	x	x	x	x	x	x	x	x	x
			x		x	x	x	x	x					x	x			x	x	x	x		x		x	x	x		x	x	x	x	x	x	x	x
	x	x	x	x	x	x	x	x	x	x			x	x	x			x	x	x	x	x			x	x	x	x				x	x			
	x	x	x	x		x	x	x	x	x	x	x	x	x	x	x	x			x	x	x	x	x	x	x	x	x	x	x	x		x	x	x	x
		x	x	x	x	x	x		x	x	x	x	x	x		x	x	x	x		x	x	x	x	x			x	x	x	x	x	x	x	x	x
		x	x	x	x	x		x	x	x	x	x								x	x	x	x	x		x		x	x	x		x	x	x	x	x
	x		x	x	x	x		x		x	x	x	x					x																		
Points																																				

touchline plan number 31

The pools are for everyone

It isn't everyone who can afford to spend a fortune on the pools. But the pools are for everyone. For only a modest stake you can still be in for the two million pounds-plus jackpot on offer every week on Littlewoods' Treble Chance pool.

But a modest stake will not go far with a full cover perm. To cover a mere twelve matches will cost you over six pounds a week.

What you want is a good plan. Here is where the series of Touch-Line plans come in. They are all registered and approved by all of the pools companies for entry as a single column of crosses.

Touch-Line Plan No. 31, for instance, is a set of a hundred single attempts spread over your own chosen sixteen matches. It costs £1.33 to send in (a mere 45 pence on Vernons), and you are guaranteed at least six in a line (possibly seven or with luck all eight) whenever you get any four top scoring draws in the top eight of your sixteen selections, plus another four in the bottom eight.

Here's a way of using it 3 times over All you have to do is put sixteen crosses anywhere in one of the right-hand Treble Chance columns, and copy the instructions alongside as shown.

Checking is quite a simple matter. All score draws score three Treble Chance points. You usually need at least five top scoring draws to win a dividend.

If you think you have a chance, list all sixteen Treble Chance values alongside the sixteen crosses on your copy coupon. Transfer them in the same order to the left hand column of all three sections of the full plan on this page.

You can now count up the total number of points you have scored with the eight crosses in each one of the hundred columns of the plan to see if any of them are winners.

Pools Trivia

Bus fitter Mick Walters was dubbed "The Most Honest Man In Britain" after splitting his £554,363 pools win with his former boss, Tom Neal. Some years before the two had decided to enter pools coupons each week and agreed they would split whatever they won. Before Mick's win they had not seen each other for more than five years, but that didn't stop him calling his old friend with the good news and spliting their fortune right down the middle.

Touchline Plan No. 31: Entry Guide

TREBLE CHANCE

ANY 2 BRACKETS FROM 3 – 3 ENTRIES OF TOUCHLINE PLAN NO 31

300 ATTEMPTS AT 4/3P = £4.00

This is an entry for a Littlewoods coupon at 4/3p per line.
The cost on Vernons would be 300 x 5/11p = £1.36
On Zetters it would cost 300 x 1/9p = £0.37

Touchline Plan No. 31 Checking Chart
Part 1

Touchline Plan No. 31 Checking Chart
Part 2

Touchline Plan No. 31 Checking Chart
Part 3

Touchline Plan No. 31 Checking Chart
Part 4

24 · touchline plan number 32

Many Guarantees With This Plan

The Treble Chance pool, with its weekly offer of a two million pounds-plus jackpot, is probably the best form of popular competition ever devised.

The odds are too long to make it in any way addictive, so all the family can join in. Pound for pound, everyone has an equal chance. You can choose any numbers you like, so you are the master of your own destiny.

A registered plan has the advantage over a full cover perm that it spreads the dividends to give you more winning weeks. A plan usually carries a guarantee, but Touch-Line Plan No. 32 is better. It has several good guarantees.

It is basically a set of 72 single attempts, spread over eighteen matches in a carefully calculated way. Any ten top scoring draws among the top twelve, or the bottom twelve, or the top six plus bottom six selections, will win you a top dividend.

Any eight top scoring draws among the top nine or bottom nine, or odd nine or even nine of the eighteen matches covered, will also in you a top dividend. There are also many other ways of winning dividends.

Here is a way of using this plan seven times to cover 21 matches at a cost on Littlewoods' coupon of £6.72 (£2.31 on Vernons at 5/11ths of a penny a go; or 84 pence on Zetters at their prize plus stake of six goes a penny).

Put 21 crosses in one of the right-hand columns against the 21 games you have chosen. Bracket them up into groups of three crosses so that you have seven brackets. Copy the instructions alongside as shown to complete your entry.

You now get all of these guarantees seven times over. For a quick check, first circle all correct one-all jackpot draws on your copy coupon and pick out your best six brackets.

List the 21 Treble Chance values for these six brackets down the side of both sections of the full plan on this page.

You can now count up the number of points you have scored with the eight crosses in each one of the 72 columns of the plan, to see if any of them are winners.

Touchline Plan No. 32: Entry Guide

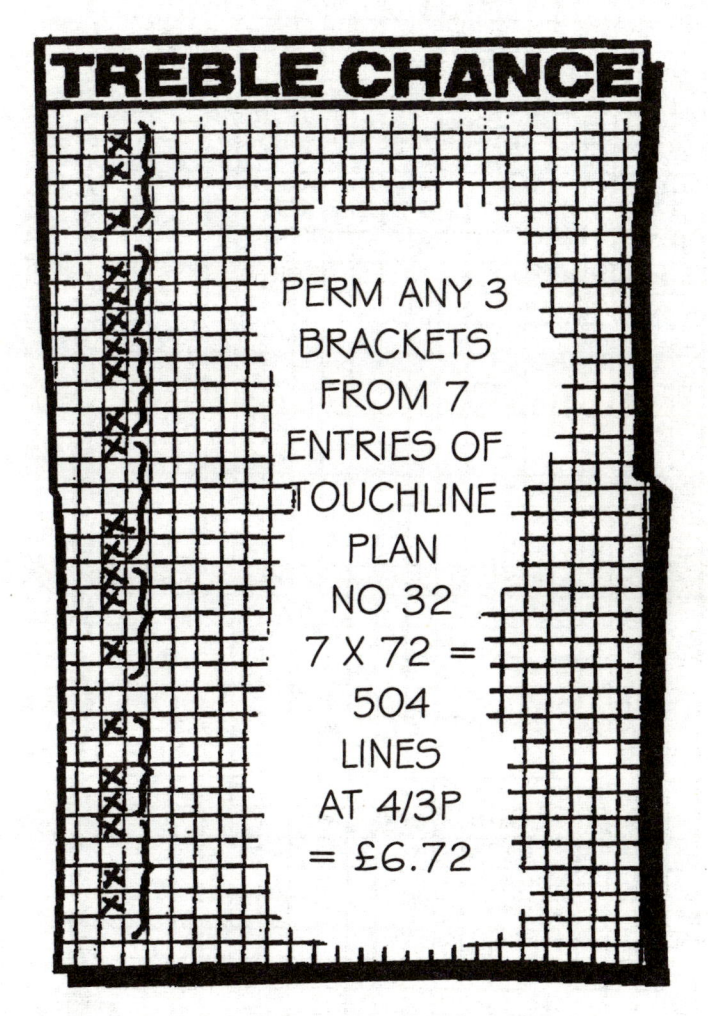

TREBLE CHANCE

PERM ANY 3 BRACKETS FROM 7 ENTRIES OF TOUCHLINE PLAN NO 32
7 X 72 = 504 LINES AT 4/3P = £6.72

This is an entry for a Littlewoods coupon at 4/3p per line.
The cost on Vernons would be 504 x 5/11p = £2.29
On Zetters it would cost 504 x 1/9p = £0.56

Results	1	2	3	4	5	6	7	8	9	10	11	12	13	14	15	16	17	18	19	20	21	22	23	24	25	26	27	28	29	30	31	32	33	34	35	36
	x				x											x	x		x			x	x	x												
		x			x	x		x		x	x	x	x			x		x				x	x	x												
			x			x	x		x			x	x	x					x	x			x	x												
			x	x			x	x		x			x	x	x	x	x	x	x	x	x	x	x	x												
			x	x	x		x	x	x		x			x	x	x	x			x			x	x	x											
	x	x	x	x	x	x	x	x	x	x		x			x							x			x	x	x	x	x							
				x	x	x	x	x	x	x															x	x	x	x	x	x	x					
					x	x	x	x	x	x	x														x	x	x	x	x	x	x	x				
	x		x	x	x					x	x	x														x	x	x	x	x	x	x	x	x		
												x																x	x	x	x	x	x	x	x	
		x	x			x						x	x	x													x		x	x	x	x	x	x	x	x
	x	x	x										x	x	x	x	x	x							x	x	x	x	x	x	x	x	x	x	x	x
														x	x	x		x	x	x	x	x	x		x		x	x		x	x	x	x	x		x
														x	x	x	x	x	x	x	x	x			x			x	x					x	x	x
						x		x	x	x			x	x	x		x	x	x	x	x	x	x	x		x	x	x		x				x	x	
														x	x	x			x	x	x	x	x				x			x	x		x	x		x
Points																																					

Touchline Plan No. 32 Checking Chart part 1

Touchline Plan No. 32 Checking Chart part 2

Results	37	38	39	40	41	42	43	44	45	46	47	48	49	50	51	52	53	54	55	56	57	58	59	60	61	62	63	64	65	66	67	68	69	70	71	72
		×							×															×					×	×	×	×	×	×	×	
	×	×						×	×														×	×				×	×		×	×	×	×	×	
	×	×	×				×	×	×													×	×				×	×		×	×		×	×	×	
	×	×	×	×			×	×	×												×	×				×		×		×	×	×		×	×	
	×	×	×	×	×		×	×	×											×	×				×	×		×	×	×		×	×		×	
	×	×	×	×	×	×	×	×	×										×	×				×		×		×		×	×		×	×	×	
	×	×	×	×	×	×	×	×										×	×				×		×		×		×	×	×	×		×	×	
	×	×	×	×	×	×	×										×	×				×		×		×		×	×	×		×	×	×	×	
	×							×								×	×				×		×		×		×		×	×	×	×	×	×		
										×	×	×	×	×	×	×	×	×																	
										×	×	×	×	×	×	×	×		×																
										×	×	×	×	×	×	×				×															
										×	×	×	×	×	×						×														
										×	×	×	×	×								×													
										×	×	×	×										×												
										×	×	×												×											
										×	×														×										
										×																×									
Points																																				

25 — touchline plan number 33

Sport A Fiver On This Plan

This entry covers twenty matches, and it involves five entries of Touch-Line Plan No. 33. For this entry you need Littlewoods' full coupon, not the short version. Put 20 crosses in a single right-hand column on the coupon and bracket them up into groups of four crosses so that you have five brackets.

Copy the instructions and stakes from the diagram on to your coupon and your entry is complete. For Vernons' coupon at 5/11p, alter the stakes to 5 x 34p = £1.70. For Zetters' coupon you write either "at 1/6p, 5 x 12p = 60p" or "at 1/9p, 5 x 8p = 40p."

You have now filled in five entries of Touch-Line Plan No. 33. This means that if you get any four score draws in the top eight plus bottom eight or odd eight plus even eight of the sixteen crosses in the best four of your five brackets, one of the 375 attempts you have sent in will include at least six, possibly seven or with luck even all eight of them.

Check by first circling all correct score draws on your copy coupon. The numbers are widely published over the weekend. You can now pick out your best four brackets.

If you think you could be a winner, list the sixteen Treble Chance values for these four brackets down the side of all three sections of the full plan on this page.

You can now count up the number of Treble Chance points you have scored with the eight crosses in each one of the 75 columns of the plan to see if any of them are winners.

Littlewoods normally pay dividends down to 21 points.

Pools Trivia

A yorkshire housewife was so broke she only had 40p left in her purse when her pools collector came to call and she normally did an entry of three 8 from 10s, costing £1.20. She was about to turn him away when her unemployed husband managed to scrape together the other 80p. His loose change ended up netting them £1,010,172

Touchline Plan No. 33: Entry Guide

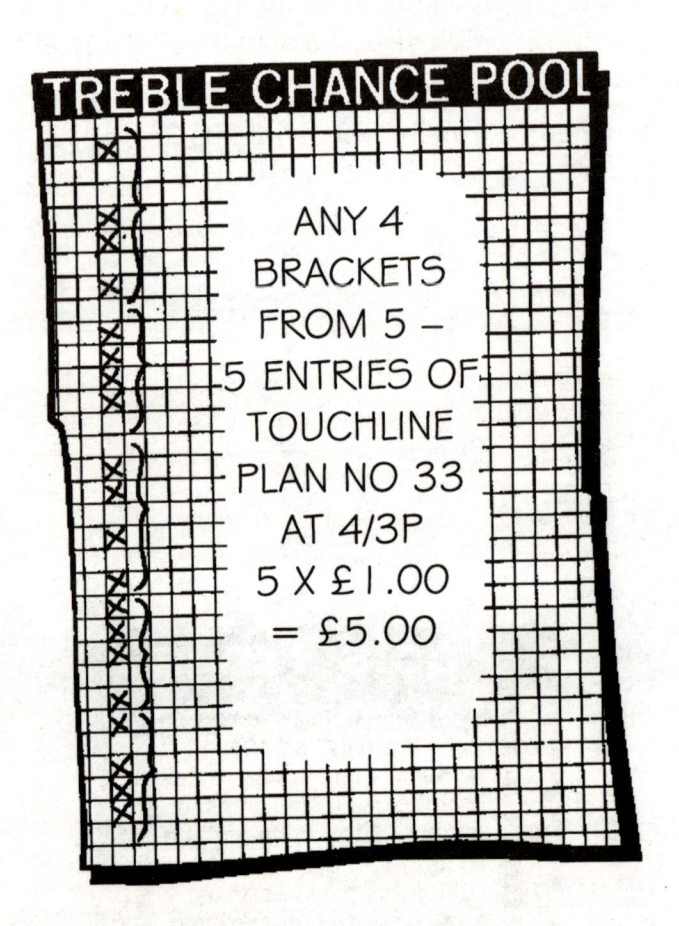

TREBLE CHANCE POOL

ANY 4 BRACKETS FROM 5 –
5 ENTRIES OF TOUCHLINE PLAN NO 33
AT 4/3P
5 X £1.00
= £5.00

This is an entry for a Littlewoods coupon at 4/3p per line.
The cost on Vernons would be 375 x 5/11p = £1.70
On Zetters it would cost 375 x 1/9p = £0.40

Touchline Plan No. 33 Checking Chart part 1

Touchline Plan No. 33 Checking Chart part 2

Touchline Plan No. 33 Checking Chart part 3

Results	51	52	53	54	55	56	57	58	59	60	61	62	63	64	65	66	67	68	69	70	71	72	73	74	75
	X	X	X	X																					
	X				X	X	X				X	X	X				X	X	X						X
					X	X	X	X	X	X	X	X	X	X	X										
			X	X		X		X	X		X		X	X			X		X	X					X
																X	X	X	X	X	X	X		
			X	X				X	X	X				X	X	X			X	X		X		
X	X	X	X											X	X	X	X	X	X	X				
X			X		X	X			X		X	X			X		X	X			X	X		X	
			X	X	X	X	X	X	X	X	X	X	X		X						X	X			
	X	X		X			X	X		X			X	X	X			X	X		X	X	X		
X	X	X	X	X	X	X	X	X	X						X	X	X	X	X	X	X				
X	X			X		X	X		X		X	X		X			X	X		X	X	X	X		
			X	X	X	X	X	X	X	X	X	X	X										X		
	X	X			X	X			X			X	X		X		X	X					X	X
X	X	X	X					X	X	X	X	X	X	X	X	X	X	X		X					
X		X	X		X		X	X		X		X	X		X		X	X		X	X		
Points																									

Pools Trivia

Alan Hepden, a heating engineer from Witney in Oxfordshire, set a new record of £1,505,443 in January 1990, using an 8 from 10 perm. Within a matter of days he was back at work as a plumber/heating engineer, saying: "I can't let my customers down. They're relying on me.

26 touchline plan number 35

There Is No Better Way

If you want to have a good go at winning the pools, there is no better way than a planned entry on a low stake coupon.

For example, this entry covers no fewer than thirty matches. It will cost you either two pounds on Zetters' coupon at nine goes a penny, or three pounds with the benefit of their prize plus stake of six goes a penny - which pays one and a half times all of the declared dividends.

On Littlewoods' coupon the corresponding stake at 1-1/3rd pence is £24, but you can always get a few friends to join in with you. Vernons' total stake at 5/11ths of a penny is £8.18.

Put 30 crosses in one of the right-hand Treble Chance columns and bracket them up into three tens. Copy the instructions alongside as illustrated. You have now filled in three entries of Touch-Line Plan No. 35, a total of 1,800 attempts.

You get these guarantees. Fourteen top scoring draws in any two brackets will win you at least one top dividend. With twelve top scoring draws, you must win at least two top or lesser dividends.

With ten top scoring draws in any two brackets, you must have at least six lines with six top scoring draws, any of which could win you a dividend depending on the results of the other two games in those lines.

You check three times: first for brackets 1 and 2, then for brackets 1 and 3, and finally with brackets 2 and 3. Then you check each resulting set of twenty selections against every column of the checking chart.

If in any one column of the checking chart you have eight or more top scoring draws, the entry wins at least one first dividend plus multiple minor dividends. With seven top scoring draws your entry wins at least three minor dividends.

If you are a winner you can depend on the pools company to find all winning lines and send you all of the dividends you have won. You must however check you brackets in the order in which they appear on the coupon.

Touchline Plan No. 35: Entry Guide

ANY 2 BRACKETS FROM 3 - 3 ENTRIES OF TOUCH-LINE PLAN NO. 35. 1,800 ATTEMPTS AT 1/9p = £2.00.

This is an entry for a Zetters coupon at 1/9p per line.
The cost on Vernons would be 1800 x 5/11p = £8.18
On Littlewoods it would cost 1800 x 4/3p = £24.00

Touchline Plan No. 35 Checking Chart

Results	1	2	3	4	5	6	7	8
	X		X		X		X	X
	X		X		X		X	X
	X		X		X		X	X
	X		X		X		X	X
	X			X		X	X	
	X			X		X	X	
	X			X		X		X
	X			X		X		X
		X	X		X	X		X
		X	X		X		X	
		X	X			X	X	
		X	X	X				X
		X	X	X				
		X	X	X				
		X			X	X		X
		X			X	X	X	
		X		X		X	X	X
	X	X				X		
	X	X			X			
	X				X	X		

FULL COVER
PERMS –
2 COLUMNS
ANY 8 FROM 11:
6 COLUMNS
ANY 8 FROM 10

touchline plan number 36

No Need to Claim If You Win

The pools companies are forever telling us that if you fail to send in your coupon you are missing your chance to win a fortune.

They also remind us that there is no need to claim when you win. They guarantee that they will check your entry every week individually and send you your cheque as soon as you win.

It is true that you are invited to claim if you are lucky enough to have scored maximum possible points. But that is only a precaution against they very remote risk of a missed top winner. In my past experience as a checker an all-correct entry sticks out a mile, so the risk is virtually non-existent.

Here is an entry that will cost you £3.30 on Zetters' Treble Chance pool at 900 shots for a pound. It uses Touch-Line Plan No. 36 which is excellent value for money.

It is a combination of six full cover perms of any eight selections from twelve, evenly spread over 24 matches in the most efficient manner possible.

To fill in your coupon you put 24 crosses in a single column against your own choice of 24 matches you hope will capture the maximum of three points for a score draw. Add the instructions and stakes alongside to complete your entry.

Alternatively you can put your 24 crosses in column A to the left of the matches plus another cross in the staking box with the name of the plan (Touch-line Plan No. 36) in the space provided at the bottom. Indicate your stake choice by marking 'X' in the box under "9-a-1p" to complete your entry.

To find your best score, list your 24 Treble Chance values down the side of the full checking plan. Pick out the column of twelve values with the most correct score draws in it and total up the best eight values in that column.

On Vernons' coupon at 5/11ths of a penny, this entry will cost you £13.50. Littlewoods' total stake at 1-1/3rd pence is £39.60.

Entry Guide

TREBLE CHANCE

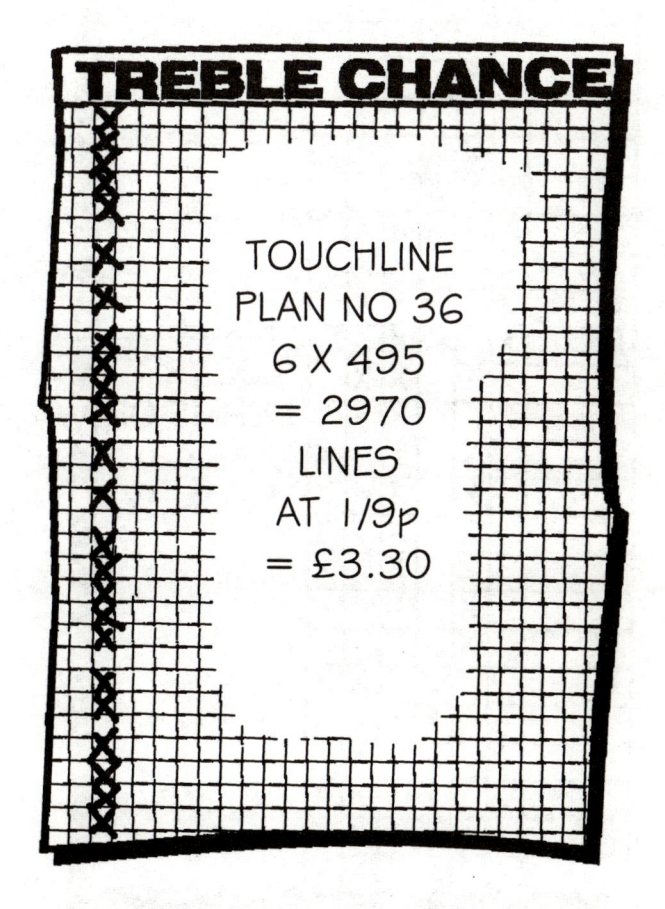

TOUCHLINE
PLAN NO 36
6 X 495
= 2970
LINES
AT 1/9p
= £3.30

This is an entry for a Zetters coupon at 1/9p per line.
The cost on Vernons would be 2970 x 5/11p = £13.50
On Zetters it would cost 2970 x 4/3p = £39.60

Results	1	2	3	4	5	6
	X	X	X			
	X	X	X			
	X	X	X			
	X	X	X			
	X	X	X			
	X	X	X			
	X			X	X	
	X			X	X	
	X			X	X	
	X			X	X	
	X			X	X	
	X			X	X	
		X		X		X
		X		X		X
		X		X		X
		X		X		X
		X		X		X
		X		X		X
			X		X	X
			X		X	X
			X		X	X
			X		X	X
			X		X	X
			X		X	X

SIX FULL COVER PERMS OF ANY 8 FROM 12

touchline block B

A Block Perm Is A Good Idea

One of the best ways of covering a large number of selections on the Treble Chance, is to use a block perm. The basic idea is that you set up two blocks of selections with four selections in each column.

Then by combining each column of one block in turn with each column of the other block, you get an entry with eight selections in each column as required by the pool rules.

You can enlarge your field of selections still further by using a multiple block perm.

For example, here is an entry costing £4.80 on Littlewoods' jackpot pool at 1-1/3rd pence for each attempt (£1.64 on Vernons at 5/11ths of a penny, or on Zetters 40 pence at nine goes a penny).

In this way you can cover a massive 40 matches of your own choice. Mark them on the coupon by putting 32 crosses in one of the right-hand Treble Chance columns.

Bracket them up into groups of eight crosses so that you have five brackets. Copy the instructions alongside as illustrated. You have now filled in 360 attempts to win a dividend.

The entry uses ready-made Touch-Line Block B, which has been specially designed to ensure that if you get any four top scoring draws out of the eight matches in any one bracket, then at least three - or with luck even all four - of them will fall together in one of the six columns of the block.

You do not need to check all of the 360 attempts you have sent in. First you circle all correct one-all jackpot draws on your copy coupon.

Pick out your best two brackets. List the Treble Chance values for the eight crosses in each of these two brackets down the side of the two full blocks on this page, using one block for each bracket.

Count up the total number of points you have scored with the four crosses in each one of the six columns of each block. Write the totals at the bottom. Circle the best total in each block.

You best score for the whole entry in the sum total of these two circled totals added together.

Entry Guide

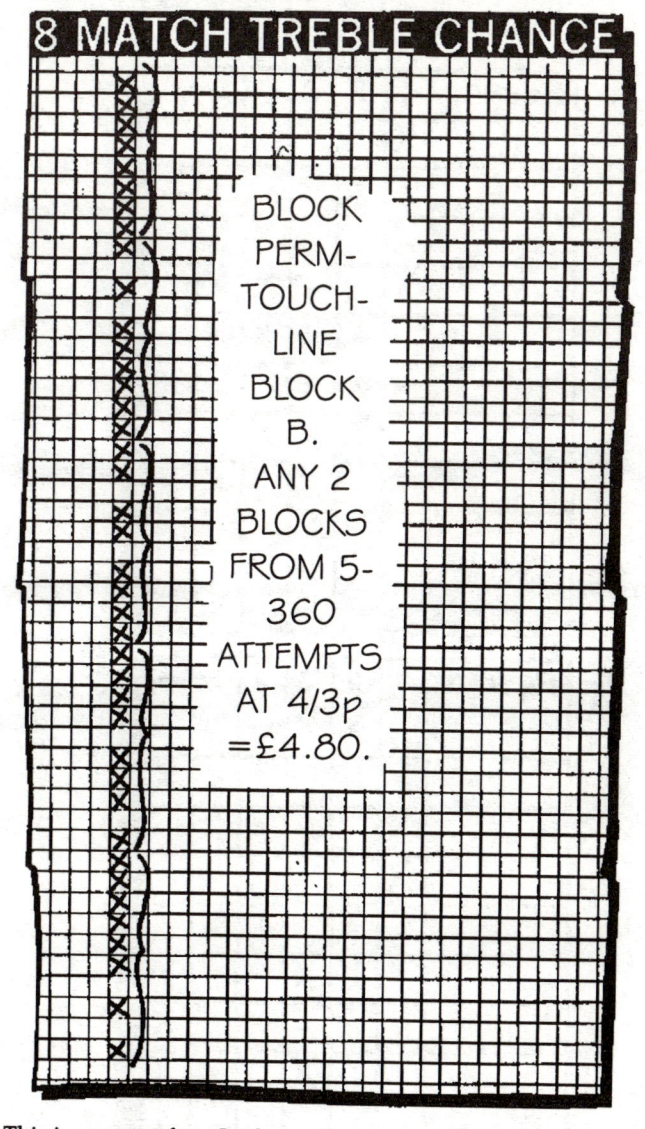

8 MATCH TREBLE CHANCE

BLOCK PERM-TOUCH-LINE BLOCK B. ANY 2 BLOCKS FROM 5- 360 ATTEMPTS AT 4/3p = £4.80.

This is an entry for a Littlewoods coupon at 4/3p per line.
The cost on Vernons would be 360 x 5/11p = £1.64
On Zetters it would cost 360 x 1/9p = £0.40

Touchline Block B Checking Chart

Results	1	2	3	4	5	6
	X	X	X			
	X	X				X
	X			X	X	
	X			X	X	
		X		X	X	
		X	X			X
			X	X		X
			X		X	X
Points						

Results	1	2	3	4	5	6
	X	X	X			
	X	X				X
	X			X	X	
	X			X	X	
		X		X	X	
		X	X			X
			X	X		X
			X		X	X
Points						

29 *touchline block C*

Steer A Middle Course

Littlewoods' Treble Chance pool, that pays the biggest dividends, has a minimum stake of one and a third pence for each attempt. On Zetters at the other end of the scale you can have as many as nine goes for a penny.

Many people like to steer a middle course. You can still win as much as half a million pounds on Vernons' coupon with a minimum stake of five elevenths of a penny for each attempt.

If you want to cover a fair number of matches you will probably get the best value for money with a block perm. Touch-Line Block C, for example, has been approved by all of the pools companies. They will accept it in the short form of a single column of crosses.

Here is a way of using three of these blocks on Vernons' coupon for a total weekly stake of £1.96 (or £5.76 on Littlewoods or just 48 pence on Zetters).

Put 27 crosses all in the same right-hand column against your own chosen 27 matches. Bear in mind that all games ending in a score draw (1-1, 2-2 etc.) will score the maximum of three Treble Chance points.

Bracket your crosses into groups of nine so that you have three brackets. Copy the instructions alongside as shown. You have now filled in 432 separate attempts to win.

If you get any six correct score draws in any two of your three brackets you must win a top dividend. There are many other ways of winning.

To check your entry, first circle all crosses on your copy coupon that have earned three points for a score draw and pick out your best two brackets.

List the Treble Chance values for the nine crosses in each of these two brackets down the side of the two blocks on this page, using one block for each bracket.

Count up the total number of points you have scored with the four crosses in each one of the twelve columns of each block. Write the totals at the bottom. Circle the best total in each block.

You can now find out how many points you have scored with the best one of the 432 attempts you have sent in. You just add together your two circled totals.

Touchline Block C: Entry Guide

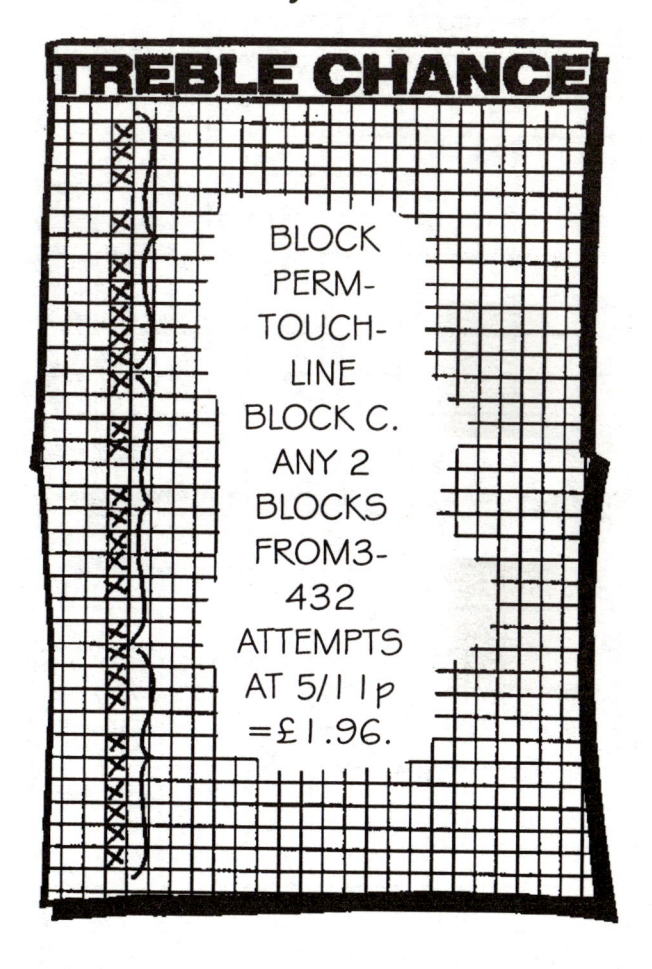

TREBLE CHANCE

BLOCK PERM-
TOUCH-
LINE
BLOCK C.
ANY 2
BLOCKS
FROM 3-
432
ATTEMPTS
AT 5/11p
= £1.96.

This is an entry for a Vernons coupon at 5/11p per line.
The cost on Littlwoods would be 432 x 4/3p = £5.76
On Zetters it would cost 432 x 1/9p = £0.48

Touchline Block C Checking Chart

Results	1	2	3	4	5	6	7	8	9	10	11	12
	X	X	X	X	X	X						
	X	X					X	X	X			
	X		X				X			X	X	
	X			X	X			X		X		X
		X	X			X		X		X		X
		X		X			X		X	X		
			X	X			X				X	X
					X	X		X	X		X	
					X	X			X		X	X
Points												

Results	1	2	3	4	5	6	7	8	9	10	11	12
	X	X	X	X	X	X						
	X	X					X	X	X			
	X		X				X			X	X	
	X			X	X			X		X		X
		X	X			X		X		X		X
		X		X			X		X	X		
			X	X			X				X	X
					X	X		X	X		X	
					X	X			X		X	X
Points												

30 touchline block D

It Sticks Out A Mile

Even if you are lucky enough to qualify for a million pound plus top dividend your claim is merely safeguarding the pools company against the risk of a missed winner.

This risk is highly unlikely because I know from my earlier experience as a pools checker that such an entry sticks out a mile and it cannot be missed.

So I suggest that you have a go at this blocks perm that will cost you £3.24 a week on Littlewoods' coupon, £1.10 on Vernons or 27 pence on Zetters.

A block perm consists typically of two blocks each being a set of columns of four crosses. Each column of the other block to make up an entry that has eight crosses in each attempt as required by the Treble Chance rules.

All Touch-Line blocks are accepted in abbreviated form as shown in this example that uses Touch-Line Block D four times, two blocks at a time.

You put 36 crosses in one of the right-hand columns of the full coupon (not the short coupon) and bracket them into groups of nine crosses so that you have four brackets.

Copy the instructions alongside as shown. You have now filled in 486 attempts. If you get any four correct score draws in any two of your four blocks, one of these 486 attempts will include at least six of them, possibly seven of with luck all eight.

You can check your best two blocks by lining up the two brackets of nine treble Chance scores against the two best columns, one from each block, added together.

Touchline Block D: Entry Guide

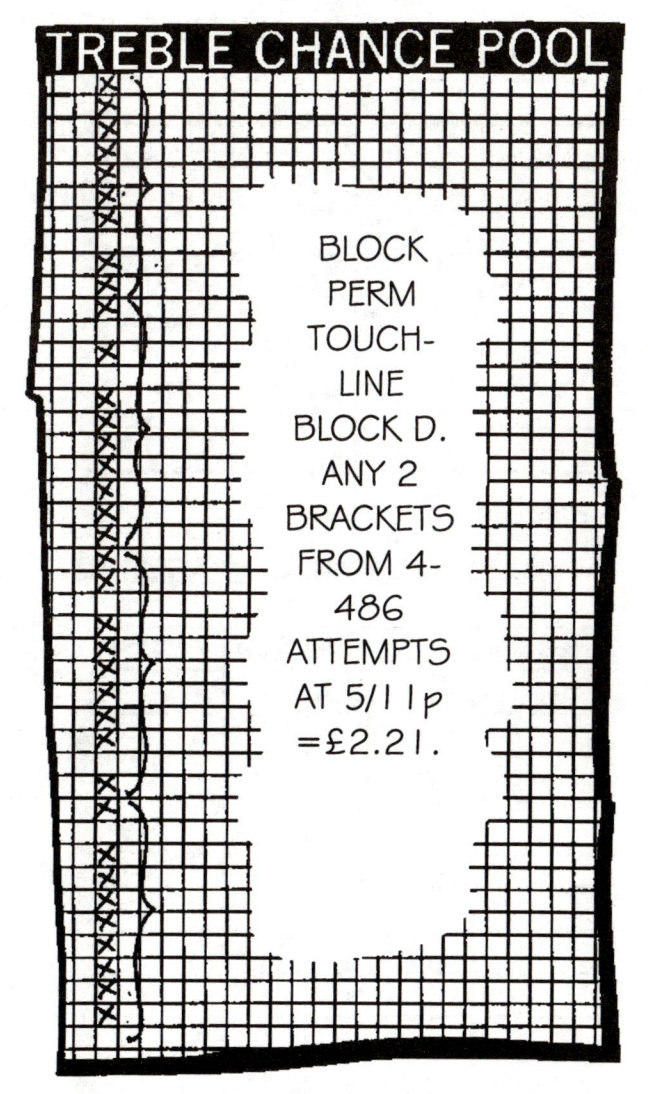

TREBLE CHANCE POOL

BLOCK PERM TOUCHLINE BLOCK D. ANY 2 BRACKETS FROM 4-486 ATTEMPTS AT 5/11p =£2.21.

This is an entry for a Vernons coupon at 5/11p per line.
The cost on Littlewoods would be 486 x 4/3p = £6.48
On Zetters it would cost 486 x 1/9p = £0.54

Touchline Block D Checking Chart

Results	1	2	3	4	5	6	7	8	9
	X	X	X	X					
	X				X	X	X		
	X	X	X					X	
	X	X	X						X
					X	X		X	X
			X		X	X	X		
		X			X	X	X		
				X		X		X	X
				X			X	X	X
Points									

Results	1	2	3	4	5	6	7	8	9
	X	X	X	X					
	X				X	X	X		
	X	X	X					X	
	X	X	X						X
					X	X		X	X
			X		X	X	X		
		X			X	X	X		
				X		X		X	X
				X			X	X	X
Points									

touchline block E

You Get What You Pay For

Penny for penny and pound for pound, all entry systems and plans for the Treble Chance pool are equal in value. You get what you pay for.

But I have always advocated a spreadover system covering a fair number of matches because to begin with you have to include some of the less likely score draws that tend to boost the dividends when they turn up as they often do. Furthermore you spread any winning dividends over more weeks so that you win more often.

So here is an example of a plan for Littlewoods coupon that covers 16 matches for £2.61 at 75 goes for a pound. Of course you can always use it on Vernons coupon at 220 shots for a pound where it will cost you £0.89. Zetters' total stake at 900 goes for a pound is 22 pence.

The plan uses Touch-Line Block E. It is a set of fourteen 'half-lines' of four selections each, spread over eight matches in such a way as to guarantee all three in a line if you get any three correct score draws among the eight matches you have chosen to be covered by the block.

The idea is to use two of these blocks and combine each half-line of one block in turn with each half-line of the other block to produce an entry made up of 196 full lines of eight selections each.

Put 16 crosses in one column and bracket them up into groups of eight crosses so that you have two brackets. Copy the instructions alongside as shown to complete your entry.

You can check it like this. First circle all correct score draws marked with a cross on your copy coupon.

List the eight Treble Chance values for the two brackets down the side of the two full blocks on this page, using one block for each bracket. Write down the total points scored by the four crosses in each column.

Your best score will be the sum of your two best totals, one from each block.

Pools Trivia

Great grandmother Peg Regan (78), of leigh-On-Sea, Essex, smashed the record payout in April 1991 with a cheque for £1,646,108.290p! She shared the win with her daughter Pauline Gooderham (50) just a week after she was robbed of £75 while out shopping at her local market.

Touchline Block E: Entry Guide

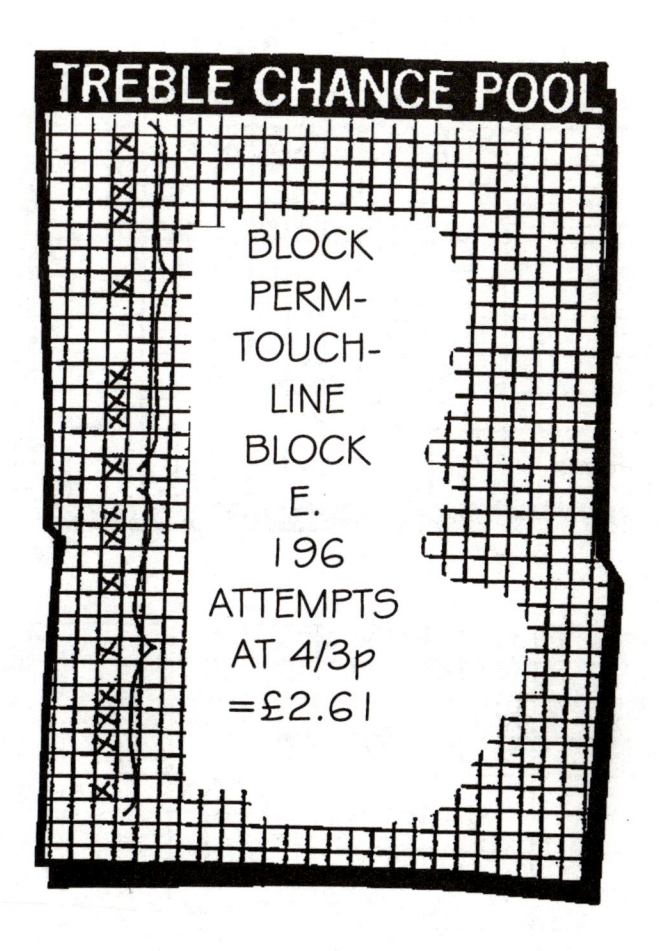

TREBLE CHANCE POOL

BLOCK PERM-
TOUCHLINE
BLOCK E.
196 ATTEMPTS
AT 4/3p
= £2.61

This is an entry for a Littlewoods coupon at 4/3p per line.
The cost on Vernons would be 196 x 5/11p = £0.89
On Zetters it would cost 196 x1/9p = £0.22

Touchline Block E Checking Chart

Results	1	2	3	4	5	6	7	8	9	10	11	12	13	14
	X	X	X				X	X	X	X				
	X	X	X								X	X	X	X
	X			X	X		X	X			X	X		
	X			X	X				X	X			X	X
		X		X		X	X		X		X		X	
		X		X		X		X		X		X		X
			X		X	X	X			X		X	X	
			X		X	X		X	X		X			X
Points														

Results	1	2	3	4	5	6	7	8	9	10	11	12	13	14
	X	X	X				X	X	X	X				
	X	X	X								X	X	X	X
	X			X	X		X	X			X	X		
	X			X	X				X	X			X	X
		X		X		X	X		X		X		X	
		X		X		X		X		X		X		X
			X		X	X	X			X		X	X	
			X		X	X		X	X		X			X
Points														

"They won a fortune on the football pools,
I believe."